The Tyne Training Ship
Wellesley
Remembered

by Brian Godfrey

The Tyne Training Ship Wellesley, formerly HMS 'Boscawen', North Shields, 22nd September 1898.

Previous page: Physical exercise for the boys of the Wellesley with the ship's band.

First published in 2014 by

Summerhill Books
PO Box 1210, Newcastle-upon-Tyne NE99 4AH

www.summerhillbooks.co.uk

email: summerhillbooks@yahoo.co.uk

ISBN: 978-1-906721-78-7

CONTENTS

An old picture postcard of the 'Wellesley tailors' at work.

The North Shields Fish Quay in Edwardian times is bustling with activity; fishing boats are clustered about the Quayside with a line of sailing ships anchored further off shore. The Wellesley, with its distinctive white bands painted around the hull, is seen at centre left of the photograph.

Acknowledgements

The author and publisher would like to thank the following who have helped with the publication of this book:

Paul (Charlie) Farley

George Nairn

Anthony Smithson, Keel Row Bookshop, North Shields

Ian Whitehead, Keeper of Maritime History, Tyne & Wear Archives & Museums

Sharyn Taylor for typing the manuscript

Bibliography

Illustrated Guide to the Tyne Training Ship 'Wellesley', 1907

TS 'Wellesley' Third Christmas Booklet, 1917

Glimpses of Old North Shields by Andrew Clark & George Nairn, 2008

By the same author

Postcards from Cramlington, 2013

Further Reading

Blyth Memories – Part Four by Jim Harland, 2013

(Includes a section on the Wellesley Nautical School at Blyth)

Introduction

The intention of this book, in part, is to validate a long held belief of mine regarding the efficacy of certain attitudes, beliefs, responses, duties and overall approach to large groups of children living in residential settings.

When I first began working in residential homes for children, the establishment was large, catering for 40 to 50 boys aged 9 to 16 years. The reason for their admittance ranged from being homeless to the crime of murder.

I feel it will be agreed that such a gathering required careful but firm management. The needs of these children were necessarily diverse and could not be met with a 'one size fits all' approach. Individual staff members would provide their own particular expertise within an overall regime that supported both children and staff. Every facet of the daily routine was designed to employ, to interest, to instil a sense of self worth and achievement and it actually worked with many children.

Apart from the naval discipline, living on an old ship in the middle of a river and the constant squawking of seagulls, there are certain strong similarities between my own experiences in residential care and the institution that was the Wellesley. The main intention of this book, however, is to celebrate, and perhaps ask a few questions of the method and motives of the mid Victorian philanthropic movements that produced new thinking in the care of children.

Brian Godfrey
April 2014

The band of the Training Ship Wellesley. Captain: H. Baynham RN. Bandmaster: J. Shutt from Scots Grey Regiment.

Background

Up until the end of the 19th century a child was considered to be the legal property of its parents. Within the 'lower classes' this allowed children to be beaten, starved, traded and actually sold for money. With the law uninterested and the rest of society complacent and accepting, it was left to individuals to voice their protests and call for a re-assessment of the importance of children within an increasingly industrialized society. By the end of the 19th century the romantic vision of England as a rural idyll with thatched cottages smothered in climbing roses, waving fields of ripening corn, buxom country girls and rosy cheeked farmers had changed. The century had culminated in England being recognised as the industrial and manufacturing heart of the world. Countless thousands deserted the countryside to seek fortune in the industrial and trading cities of the country. While the labour intensive industries of manufacturing, shipbuilding, coalmining etc provided jobs for many, many more would find a wretched, despairing life within overcrowded and squalid communities. For children growing up in such conditions and without any legal protection, their situation must have been beyond desperate. With drunkenness, prostitution and crime a daily blight within these communities, children were largely disregarded in the struggle to survive. Increasingly the plight of these children was recognised and various charitable movements began to reach out. The Poor Law had failed to address the ever increasing problem of destitute and abandoned children.

A poor boy, late 1800s.

A boy ready for sea.

Perhaps a forerunner to nautical education, though not purely in the Wellesley manner, was the Commercial and Mathematical School, Seaton Sluice that was operating during 1830s. The headmaster, Jesse Dawson, had previously been a schoolmaster at Hexham and always desired to start an academy on the coast. The Seaton Sluice establishment became so successful that branches were opened at Blyth and North Shields. The Seaton Sluice building was situated on the Quayside below the King's Arms. For simple reading and writing, the fee was seven shillings a quarter and the payment of one guinea (twenty one shillings) ensured tuition in theoretical geometry, algebra, navigation and nautical astronomy, also the construction of maps and charts. Three of the first five masters certificates ever obtained for steam vessels were won at Seaton Sluice.

It was during the period of the 1850s-80s that saw the founding of the voluntary children societies, ragged schools, industrial schools, all night shelters, village homes and of course, the most famous and enduring of all Dr Barnardo's. The good doctor opened his first home for destitute boys in London in 1870 and his name is now synonymous with child care. Barnardo's did not differentiate between these boys who had committed an offence and these simply abandoned by their parents. While the name of Thomas John Barnardo is perpetuated throughout the world – predominant in intervening in any situation where children are deemed at risk – the name of James Hall is no less celebrated in the North of England.

At this time there was also the rise of the 'fashion' for the training ship. Some of these ships were simply 'reformative' for those boys who had criminal involvement and with very little opportunity for personal advancement. Other, such as the Wellesley offered care, training, discipline, and the opportunity to make a life other than the one the boys had known. Recognising the need for a more philanthropic approach to the homeless and neglected boys of Tyneside, Mr Hall in 1867 called for the establishment of an industrial training ship on the Tyne. A philanthropist and also a 'canny' businessman, he recognised that the mercantile marine of this country was suffering through lack of well trained seamen. Therefore his school would attempt to solve this problem through giving these boys a new life and an honourable purpose. Mr Hall gained support for these ventures from leading businessmen throughout the area and he personally approached the Admiralty to secure the ship for the purpose. Their Lordships were willing to allow the use of the frigate 'Diana' of 1083 tons register to be fitted out and towed to the Tyne from Chatham at the expense of the institution. The expense was found to be too great and another vessel was secured. The 'Cornwall' had been a reformatory ship moored on the Thames. The ship's trustees applied for and received a larger vessel and wanted it to retain the name 'Cornwall'. The old 'Cornwall' was with permission from the Admiralty renamed Wellesley and towed to the Tyne, arriving on 11th June 1868.

James Hall founder of the Wellesley Training Ship.

The 'Old Wellesley' was moored opposite the Coble Dene on the Tyne. She was formally opened for the reception of boys by his grace the Duke of Northumberland in the presence of many local dignitaries on 30th July 1868. Considering that the proposal to form the Society was made only in January of the same year, no time appears to have been lost in realising the objective. The goal was to establish a school ship on the Tyne '*for the reception of boys, who through poverty, parental neglect, or being orphans, or from any other cause are left destitute and homeless and in danger of contamination from association with vice and crime, and the training such boys to a sea faring life.*' These admirable sentiments were expressed in a speech given to a public meeting on 17th January 1868 by Mr James Hall JP of Tynemouth. It is felt that Mr Hall, through enlisting the support and patronage of influential people including Lords, MPs and church men, was solely responsible for bringing such a needed project to Tyneside. Throughout his involvement with the Wellesley, James Hall displayed great enthusiastic and solid belief in the cause of prospering the lives of disadvantaged boys in Tyneside.

The Wellesley was licensed under the Industrial Schools Act of 1866, for the accommodation of 200 boys; under the terms of the licence this number could not be increased. In placing the ship under the Act, clause 36 allowed a maintenance payment by HM Treasury of five shillings per boy per week.

Later, a larger vessel the 'Boscawen' was brought to the Tyne to replace the first Wellesley. Fitted out and a licence for 300 boys obtained, the 'Boscawen' was renamed Wellesley and it is this particular incarnation with which this book is concerned.

A painting showing the Wellesley off North Shields in 1896. This was the second vessel named Wellesley to be moored in the Tyne for the training of boys.

Beginnings

A familiar and welcome sight to any mariner entering the Tyne from the fearsome North Sea during the late 19th and early 20th centuries would have been the Wellesley. Moored at North Shields, her white banded hull and rows of gunports may have inspired thoughts of death dealing broadsides, shot away masts, Johnny Frenchman striking his colours after a thorough thrashing by jolly British Tars and general all round swash buckling. For the Wellesley was one of the last sailing line of battleships from the era of the 'wooden walls of England'. Launched in 1844 as the 'Boscawen', the ship was not of the Nelson era but would have been virtually indistinguishable from ships of that glorious period in British naval history. Carrying 74 guns, which would still have to be muzzle loaded, the 'Boscawen' saw Foreign Service on the West Coast of Africa and Cape of Good Hope stations. After just 16 years service she was paid off at Devonport, stripped of her armament and anything else that was useful, leaving her a hulk.

By 1873 the old Wellesley was classed as the smallest of the school ships operating in the river estuaries of England. She had a complement of 240 boys at this time but the committee wanted to increase this number to 300, the maximum allowed by government regulation so this of course required a larger vessel. The Wellesley Executive Committee, having been offered the old 'Boscawen' by the Admiralty, needed to find at least £4,000 to transform the cut-down hulked ship into the icon of the Tyne – the Wellesley. Through generous donations and financial backing by prominent political and pastoral figures, the sum was realised within a fairly short time. A licence was thus obtained from the Home Office for the reception of 300 boys.

The old 'Boscawen' now renamed Wellesley was converted and refurbished in accordance with the stipulations for such vessels, set by the Reformatory Committee on the Thames, however, the Wellesley not only met these standards but the aim was to actually improve on them. The health and well-being of the boys was seen as paramount.

ORDER SENDING CHILD TO "WELLESLEY" TRAINING SHIP.

TO WIT.

Be it remembered, That on the Day of 18 in pursuance of the Industrial Schools Act, 1866, We, Two of Her Majesty's Justices of the Peace, for the said of , do order that of who was born on the day of 18 , (whose Religious Persuasion appears to us to be), being a Child subject to the Provisions of Section of the said Act, be sent to the "Wellesley" Training Ship, Certified Industrial School at Shields, and that he be detained there until he is 16 years of age.

(Signed)

N.B.—It is particularly requested that the age may be entered as accurately as possible.

Left: A standard form used in the late 19th century for committing a boy to the Wellesley under the Industrial Schools Act of 1866.

Improved heating and ventilation and the optimum use of space below decks for accommodation, recreation and schooling were essential improvements. Diet was another area that was reviewed and the following is the menu presented to the boys aboard the Wellesley at the end of the 19th century.

Breakfast
Oatmeal porridge with milk and sugar on two mornings of the week.
Boiled rice with milk and treacle on two mornings.
1/2 pint of cocoa and 8 ozs bread on two mornings.
1/2 pint of coffee and 8 ozs bread on Sundays.

Dinner
On Sundays, Tuesdays and Thursdays,
5 ozs fresh meat with potatoes and haricot beans and suet pudding.

Mondays and Fridays,
3 ozs cold preserved meat and 1 pint of lentil soup with the addition of barley and fresh vegetables.

On Saturday
Plum pudding.

Tea
1/2 pint of tea and 8 ozs bread.
On Saturdays 4 ozs corned beef and on Sunday 1 oz of butter or marmalade.

Supper
3 ozs biscuits and 1/2 pint of cocoa.

Provisions were brought to the ship by local suppliers who no doubt could smell the 1350 lbs of bread that was baked on board each week.

Cocoa was on the menu for breakfast and supper and here is an advert for a Newcastle company that supplied 'Wellesley' brand.

The boys from the Wellesley sitting down for one of their meals in the mess deck (lower).

The boys who were sent to the Wellesley were to be of good character, in that they would have no criminal convictions or been involved in any criminal activity. The boys were to be trained in the art of seamanship while receiving '*a sound elementary education and a good moral and religious training*'. The Committee considered that in this way, the boys would be prepared for the noblest service in which an Englishman can engage – the sea service of his country. Naturally the majority of the boys came from Tyneside and the surrounding areas but some were from the North Yorkshire, Liverpool, Manchester and as far south as London. They were admitted between the ages of 12 and 16 years, at which age they would be discharged.

Boys at seamanship instruction with the chief officer.

However the entry register for Wellesley, which recorded the reasons boys were sent to the ship, is a little at odds with the professed criteria. Although the most common reasons were 'being uncontrollable', 'stealing' and 'found wandering' other, far more serious offences, are recorded.

Shop and warehouse breaking, criminal and indecent assaults, malicious and wilful damage to property, an indecent assault on a nine year old girl and larceny are among the serious reason given. While having a parent with criminal habits, having no proper guardianship, escaping from a workhouse, not attending school or even damaging turnips, were some of the lesser offences that could have a boy 'sent to the hulks'.

ORDER OF DETENTION IN THE "WELLESLEY" TRAINING SHIP.

THE ELEMENTARY EDUCATION ACT, 1876.

In the County of   Petty Sessional
Division of

Before THE COURT OF SUMMARY JURISDICTION, sitting at

The   day of   189 .

Whereas an attendance order under the 11th Section of the Elementary Education Act, 1876, was made against the child
of   (born, so far as has been ascertained, on the   day of   189 ,) and who is under the said Act prohibited from being taken into full time employment on the ground that *he was found habitually wandering* [*or not under proper control*], *or in the company of rogues, vagabonds, or disorderly persons* [*or reputed criminals*], and the said attendance order has not been complied with, without any reasonable excuse within the meaning of the said Act. And whereas the *parent has satisfied the Court that he has used all reasonable efforts to enforce compliance with the said order*, said non-compliance was not the first non-compliance with the said order.

And whereas the religious persuasions of the said child appears to the Court to be that of

It is hereby ordered that the said child shall be sent to the "*Wellesley*" *Training Ship Certified Industrial School at Shields*, to be there detained until he is sixteen years of age.

We direct that the County (Borough) of
contribute to the maintenance of the said child.

Justices of the Peace for the said

Left: A standard order of detention form under the elementary Education Act of 1876. This is what was likely to happen to habitual non school attenders in the late 19th century. However, many boys were saved from a very uncertain future through the application of this order.

Right: A completed admittance form for the Wellesley under the name of John Robert Robson. John's age is not given but he was thought to be 'apparently under the age of fourteen years'. He had 'no visible means of subsistence and not having any home.' John attended Rothbury Boys School and had previously been convicted for 'putting chairs on the railway.' He could read and write and his medical checks made him physically fit for life at sea. With mother, Annie Robson dead and father, William Robson 'at present undergoing a sentence of imprisonment for starving one of his children to death.' The form is signed by surgeon 'J. Simplejack' and dated 10th February 1883.

Many years ago my own establishment had a stated criteria similar to that of the Wellesley. We would take what we called at the time 'Welfare Cases'. Children who, through no fault of their own, needed to be removed from the situation they were in to a place of safety. Alongside these children, we were asked to look after those who had committed criminal offences and who awaited a court appearance. It became a difficult task as the operating systems of the establishment could not differentiate. Routine, structure and discipline needed to be maintained for all within the establishment and segregation impossible. The thinking behind this was that the positive influence of children who had not committed crime would somehow 'rub off' on those that had and a magical transformation would take place. Those that championed this view were proved, in my experience, entirely wrong. I have seen children brought into care for non school attendance, progress to a career of car theft, burglary etc simply through being exposed to certain influences. The Wellesley ship's company then, would have been quite similar in its social composition, though much larger, than the biggest social services establishment in the 1980s.

QUESTIONS.	ANSWERS.
1.—Name?	John Robert Robson
2.—Age—Date of Birth? *	The said John Robert Robson is apparently under the age of fourteen years
3.—Religious Denomination?	Roman Catholic
4.—Has he been Baptized?	not Known
By whom, and where?	not Known
5.—With what Charged?	not having any visible means of subsistance & not having any home
6.—Previous complaints—How many, and what offences?	was convicted 5 years ago for putting Chairs on Railway
7.—Under what Section of the Act? ...	Section fourteen
8.—Previous Character?	
9.—State if Illegitimate?	no
10.—Name of Parents, or	William Robson and Annie Robson
Step Parents?	His Mother is dead and his father is at present undergoing a sentence of imprisonment for starving one of his children to death
Their Address?	
Occupation?	
Character?	
Circumstances, and Particulars? ...	
11.—Country of Father?	
Country of Mother?	
12.—Boy's place of Birth?	not known
13.—Name and Address of late Employer? ..	
14.—What School attended?	Rothbury Boys School
Can he read?	yes
Can he Write?	yes
15.—Is the boy sent at the instance of a School Board, if so, what Board? ...	no
Remarks on the Case—	

MEDICAL QUESTIONS.

QUESTIONS.	ANSWERS.
1.—Is the boy generally sound and healthy? ...	yes
2.—Of the ordinary growth and strength of a boy of his age?	yes
3.—Has he perfect use of all his limbs, his eyesight, and his hearing? ...	yes
4.—Sound Intellect?	yes
5.—Has he had the Cow Pox or Small Pox?	Has been Vaccinated
6.—Is he Scrofulous, or subject to Epileptic or other Fits?	no
7.—Is he perfectly free from Cutaneous Disorder?	Slight cutaneous eruption
8.—Is he physically fitted for a sea life?	He is

Signature of Surgeon, J. Simplejack M. B.

Date, February 10th 1883

The above Questions may be answered by the Surgeon of the Union Workhouse or House of Detention to which the boy is remanded, or by any respectable Medical Man to whom it may be convenient to refer.

The Training Ship being an *Industrial* School, no Boy can be admitted who is mentally or physically unfitted for a seafaring life.

A nice view of the Wellesley which is seen 'dressed overall'. This is a Royal Naval tradition that celebrates special occasions such as, Trafalgar Day, Ascension Day, the Monarch's birthday etc. It may be that as the postcard is dated for 1906, the ship is 'dressed overall' to celebrate the visit of Edward VII to Newcastle. The ship is rigged with flags and bunting and each yard is manned by the Wellesley boys. The tradition was only performed while a ship was in harbour.

A photograph from the 1890s showing the ship to full advantage. Sails have been removed, masts shortened and the bowsprit that would have supported the huge triangular jib sails, has also been shortened. The davits for raising and lowering the long boats can be seen on the ship's side. The boats are being used, on a very benign looking River Tyne for rowing practice. This continued right up until the early 1970s, as the Wellesley boats were a regular sight in Blyth Harbour.

This is probably one of the most famous and enduring images ever taken on the Tyne. The magnificent 'Mauretania' makes stately progress to the sea on Tuesday, 22nd October 1907. She is escorted by her tugs and a flotilla of small boats to bid the 'Old Girl', as Captain McNeil would later call her, farewell. The Wellesley is seen on the right of the picture and a strong glass reveals that the ship's company is lining the side watching the 'Mauretania' go by. No doubt the occasion would have been a welcome distraction from the daily routine aboard the Wellesley.

Training & Instruction

The boys were instructed in all aspects of seamanship – making and shortening sails, steering, wearing ship, tacking and rules to observe while at sea. A large model of a brig on a revolving stand was an aid to instructing the boys in compass reading and how the wheel and rudder affected the ship's head while underway. Sail-making classes were for senior boys and as well as sails, work suits, aprons, canvas buckets etc were made and repaired. Senior boys were also taught a *'true sailor's work'*. Terms which are archaic and almost mysterious to landsmen are used to describe what the boys needed to master, for instance does anyone know how to 'mouse a hook' or use a 'parbuckle' and can anyone perform the ancient art of 'parcelling' or 'worming'. How about knots? How are you at making a 'bight' or 'timber hitch' or 'coband hitch' or 'marlin spike hitch'. The boys were given the opportunity to apply this knowledge in the spring of each year when the masts and yards were sent aloft and re-rigged after being removed for the winter.

Boys at practical seamanship with chief instructor.

Between the hours of 9 am and 1.30 pm, what was called the *'watch out of school'* was divided into its different classes. Seamanship classes, as already mentioned, but also the more mundane but no less important skills acquired by tailors, plumbers, carpenters, shoemakers and cooks. Cleanliness also needed to be maintained and work parties to cover bathrooms, drying rooms and laundry were part of the daily routine. All boys would also take part in 'drill' parties. Although 'cutlass drill' was a little outmoded by this time. Target practice and physical drill, with or without arms, was an integral part of life onboard. Physical exercise was accompanied by the ship's band with sometimes the whole of the ship's company taking part.

Morris tube rifle practice.

Chief Government Inspector Legge reported in March 1903: *'A fine display of physical drill with and without arms was given none better to be seen on board any of our ships.'* Such displays were often given by the company, accompanied by the band at local engagements.

Boys at cutlass exercise.

Boys in the sailmaking class.

Trades such as sail making, cooking, tailoring, carpentry etc were taught as a ship at sea needed to be self-sufficient for perhaps months at a time. The importance of 'specialist' sailors aboard ship cannot be underestimated. All clothing worn by the boys with the exception of caps was made by the boys in the tailors shop. As well as uniforms, shirts, stockings, towels, pillow covers, aprons etc were also made. Not having to purchase these items from a supplier and buying only the necessary clothes, resulted in a substantial saving against purchasing finished items. A statement for the tailors shop for 1897 reads: *'Cost of materials £263.7.10$^1/_2$. Value of garments produced £487 – saving £223.12.1$^1/_2$.'*

This is quite a saving when it is remembered that each of the 300 boys needed to be outfitted with three complete suits of clothes. As with the tailor, the ship's shoemaker was responsible for making and repairing boots for both boys and officers. The shoemaker would cut out the various leather components and the boys, under direction, completed the boot using traditional hand making tools. Again, substantial savings were made here with repairs to old boots and the making of new ones – saving £143.12.9 for the year 1897. Similar savings were made throughout the ship with the boys being taught cookery, carpentry, plumbing and any other trade that would make the Wellesley virtually self sufficient in every department save that of food. Even with these savings there was concern that the Wellesley was not self sufficient financially.

Annual subscriptions to the venture and revenues derived from other public sources had, by 1897, fallen to a critical level. With an annual running cost of £6,300 for Wellesley and £973 for that of the Greens Home (an industrial school licensed as a branch of the Wellesley in South Shields), the committee was forced to use reserve funds and that which they had invested.

Shoemakers at work.

With annual running costs of over £7,000 in the late 1890s, the committee of the Wellesley were always appealing for more funds.

Right: The forms for donors to offer legacies and subscriptions for 'The Tyne Training Ship Wellesley of Homeless and Destitute Boys'.

FORM OF LEGACY.

I bequeath to the "Wellesley" Training Ship Institution for Homeless and Destitute Boys, the sum of free from Legacy duty, and I direct that the said Legacy shall be paid to the Treasurer of the said Institution for the time being, whose receipt shall be a sufficient discharge for the same. And I direct that the aforesaid Legacy to the Institution shall be paid exclusively out of such part of my personal estate as may lawfully be given by Will for Charitable purposes and in preference to all other payments thereof.

Donations and Subscriptions will be thankfully received by any Member of the Committee, the Treasurer, or the Secretary.

The Committee will be greatly obliged if SUBSCRIPTIONS can be paid as soon after the 1st JANUARY in each year as convenient.

(Kindly fill in and sign this paper, detach same, and forward it as addressed.)

Cheques to be made payable to the "Wellesley" Training Ship, and crossed Bank of England.

The Tyne Training Ship "Wellesley" for Homeless and Destitute Boys.

I authorise you to enter my name as a Donor of .... *Pounds.*

As a Subscriber of .... *Pounds.*

Name ....

Address ....

Date ....

To Mr. GEORGE LUCKLEY, Secretary, Queen Street, NEWCASTLE-ON-TYNE.

Boys of the Wellesley cooking class. On the table are signs saying: 'Meat' ... 'Spuds' ... 'Tart' ... 'Rice' ... 'Apple' and 'Pie'.

Daily Routine aboard the Wellesley

6.00 am	Boys turn out, stow beds, bedding etc silent prayers.
6.15 am	To bathroom by division, in rotation, wash decks.
7.00 am	Breakfast.
7.30 am	Muster for inspection. Shift clothing.
7.45 am	Clean mess gear and clear up decks, boat for mail and officers.
8.15 am	Physical and other drills.
8.30 am	Divisions for inspection and sick call.
8.50 am	Prayers.
9.00 am	One watch to school, the remainder to instructions, tailors, shoemakers, carpenters and plumbers to work.
11.50 am	Clean up decks.
Noon	Disperse.
0.30 pm	Dinner.
1.00 pm	Clean mess gear and clear up decks, recreation.
1.30 pm	School and instruction.
4.30 pm	Disperse and shift clothing.
5.00 pm	Officers boat leaves ship.
5.20 pm	Hands to dress.
6.00 pm	Evening school in winter. Summer routine – boys recreation field. Party away at boat exercise, party away bathing.
7.40 pm	Supper.
7.50 pm	Up tables and stools, clear up decks.
8.00 pm	Prayers in winter, 8.30 pm in summer.
9.00 pm	Boys to bed. Rounds.
10.00 pm	Out lights in officers mess room.
10.30 pm	Cabins lights out.

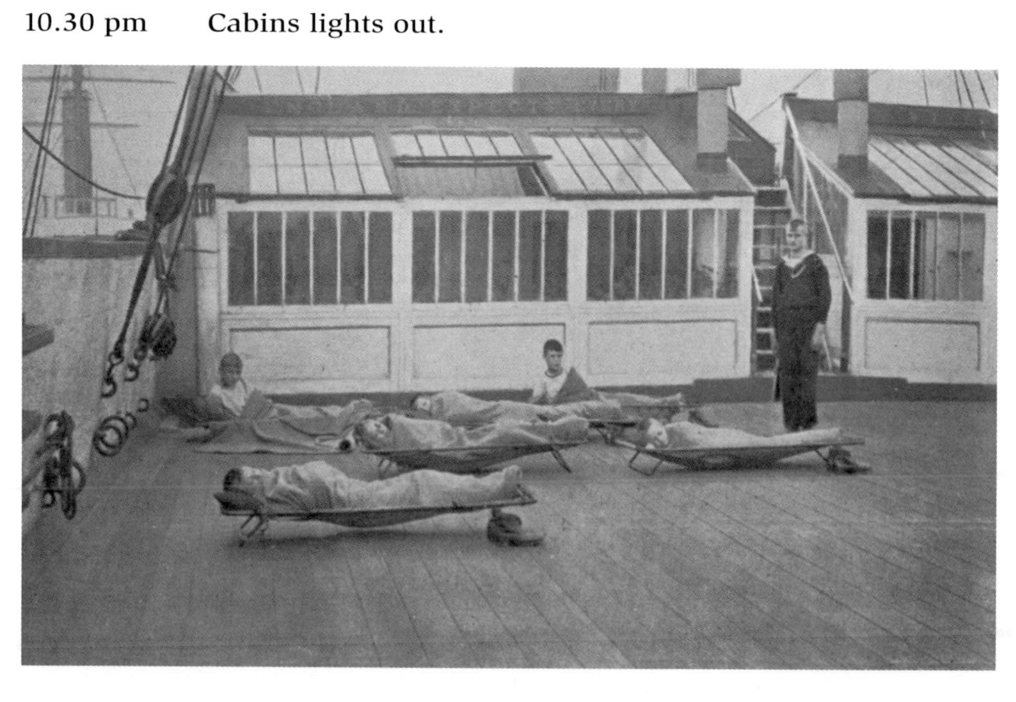

Sleeping cots used by the boys on board the Wellesley. At 9 pm the boys were expected to be in bed and by 10.30 pm the cabin lights were turned off.

Each Friday the boys received religious instruction for one hour and the choir would go to practise for one hour before supper. The Captain made his inspection each Sunday morning at 9.30 am after which the boys were taken ashore to attend their respective places of worship. Divine service was held on board also on Sunday and a bible class in the school room for those who did not wish to go ashore for a walk, after dinner.

Carpenters and plumbers at work.

The boys of the ambulance class.

As can be seen from the daily routine of the boys, no time was allowed for idleness or boredom – sadly a common affliction today. The routine was designed to serve a number of purposes based on the sound premise that too much free time will inevitably be misused. Within such an environment discipline and good order was essential for the establishment to fulfil its purpose. The Wellesley had a stated purpose and everything onboard was geared towards achieving that end. The boys who accepted this as a part of their personal development saw benefits in conduct and attitudes towards others and instilled within them a sense of comradeship and duty to others.

Comparable Social Services establishments, comparable only in the residential element, also had stated intentions towards its charges. Specialist workers work to deliver targeted care based upon individual need and within the stated purpose of rehabilitation, preparing for independence etc. In my experience children need the certainty that a regular routine brings. It is all encompassing, safe, predictable and satisfying. The onus of course is on the supervising adults to ensure that the various components are acceptable and that standards of response are maintained. There will always be, however, within any great gathering of children such as this certain personalities that are not receptive to an imposed regime, however well meaning. These children will either abscond at any opportunity or stay to pose problems within a system that cannot cater for their needs. Absconding from my own establishment was quite frequent but I cannot find any record of absconding from the Wellesley. I have no doubt that given the numbers of children involved some would have responded favourably to the discipline imposed aboard the ship. The opportunities to abscond from a ship moored fifty yards or so from dockside would have been few. Shore parties would have been a golden opportunity but any boy with the idea of running away in mind, would probably be known by the rest of his division. Peer pressure is a very effective agent. Given the social conditions and the sometimes desperate circumstances in which a lot of the boys were born into, it is not surprising most chose to stay within an environment that fed and clothed and rewarded endeavour. Modern thinking sees the kind of regime as operated on the Wellesley and others of a far less expectant nature, as a violation of rights, verging on child abuse. Wellesley boys were renowned for their good conduct and sense of duty. Nowhere is this better illustrated than in the Wellesley Roll of Honour.

Physical Exercise

Physical exercise was an important part of the regime on the Wellesley. Above is the gymnastic class with chief officer.

The Wellesley football team.

Here the boys take part in a dumb-bell exercise.

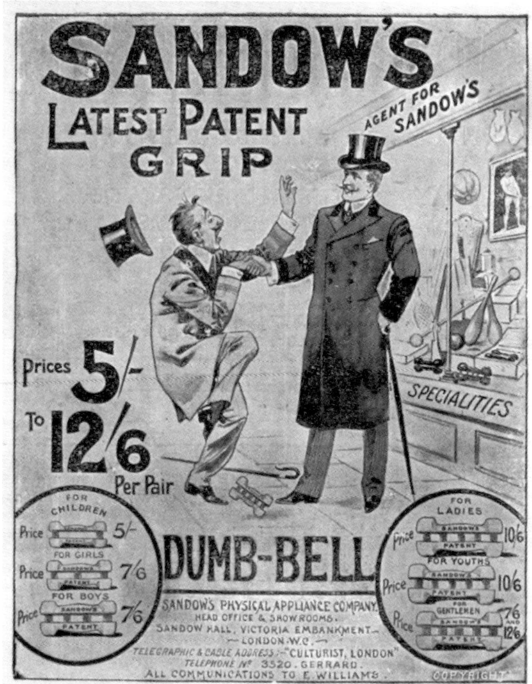

An advert for the dumb-bells 'used aboard the Wellesley' and seen being used by the boys in the photograph on the left.

Greens Home

Greens Home in South Shields derived its name from the Rev Robert Green who was vicar of Longhorsley in Northumberland for over 50 years. The reverend occupied the house with his sisters and died in 1877, but not before giving the house to the Wellesley Committee. The initial idea was to provide accommodation for old Wellesley boys returning from sea. However, for reasons not revealed this project was not a success and the building was used as a hospital for a short period. The use of the building changed again when the committee decided in 1885 to open an industrial school, as a fully licensed branch of the Wellesley. The home was to serve as a reception establishment for 60 boys, with the same stipulation as that of the Wellesley, boys had to be unconvicted of crime. The idea being to take in boys at an earlier age, that of 6 years, begin their education and then transfer to the ship at 12 years of age. The boys received into Greens Home were thought to be '*physically, mentally or morally below the average and in many cases below the average in all three points.*' Obviously boys such as these, coming from desperately destitute situations required nourishment and their menu would have been based upon that of the Wellesley. This combined with the '*Victorian panacea*' of regular and vigorous exercise soon had the little chaps '*ship shape*'.

My own experience in the residential care of boys confirms these ideas. Boys were brought to us who were clearly in need of '*beefing up*' and whose moral and mental conditions required development. One boy in particular would recoil in horror on being presented with a hot meal. A particular trial was his first traditional Sunday lunch; the young chap, could not understand that the '*big pile of white stuff*' was mashed potato and that '*the long orange things*' were carrots. He had been used to bare slices of bread, crisps, biscuits etc with the consequence that he required instruction in the use of a knife and fork at 14 years of age. It must be remembered that boys such as this were very often treated harshly by their fellows. They had few friends and the other boys would give them the name of '*starvers*'. Initially reviled and mocked they would eventually be accepted by the others but would remain low in the pecking order that naturally develops within such societies.

No doubt the boys who entered Greens Home for the first time would have met similar conditions. However, with care and firmness and given time, a tolerable transformation takes place. A Government Inspector's report on Greens Home in 1896 stated that '*The little charges here are full of life and spirit, and seem thoroughly happy, they are carefully looked after in every way, and their intelligence is well developed.*' This corresponds with my own experience within residential care. The needs of the boys within Greens Home were thought to be met best through regular meals and exercise, moral development and education. Mr J.G. Legge, Home Officer Inspector reported '*The school is a capital specimen of a junior school and shows what can be done in this direction.*' As an extension of the Wellesley, in the early 1900s the home was under the superintendence of Captain Baynham but was in the charge of Mr A. Shearlaw, who lived on the premises. Education at the Home was under the overall control of the Wellesley Headmaster and delivered by Mr Murray.

The Band

The Wellesley ship's band was treated as a separate division within the ship and in the early 1900s was under the command of the band master, Mr Shutt. He himself was an old Wellesley boy who went on to serve in the Royal Scots Regiment. For obvious reasons the band room aboard Wellesley was situated at the furthest extremity of the ship. The boys were not exempt from any of the rigours faced by their fellows in other divisions, having to practice their instruments while attending to school work.

Consisting of thirty performing members, the band also had a further twenty boys under tuition as a reserve. These boys, when thought able, would fill any place in the main band vacated through discharges. Over the years the band managed to build a reputation throughout Tyneside and beyond, for its performances and smart turnout. The band could be engaged to play at parades, festivals, shows, garden parties on the vicarage lawn and concerts, and for a small extra charge a hornpipe dancer.

A contingent of Wellesley boys and the band took part in the welcoming parade for the King's visit to Newcastle in 1906.

As well as improving their technical and artistic abilities with their chosen instruments, through regular practice and performances, it was felt that '*The moral tone of boys instructed in music is naturally raised.*'

There are many testaments regarding boys who had been trained and instructed in music aboard the Wellesley. These boys had become bandsmen in Naval and Army bands and prompted tributes like:

'*Bandsman George Barker is a good and willing solider, an excellent musician, and is worthy the ship he came from.*' Bandmaster of the Buffs

'*I am pleased to inform you that three boys I had from you recently are going on very well indeed, in fact they quite lick any of the other lads.*'
Bandmaster of the Royal Warwick Regiment

'*I have much pleasure in stating, with reference to the boy R. Robinson that his conduct and attention to work is all that could be desired.*' Colonel 2nd Royal Irish Rifles

The ship's band is gathered on the fore deck for this formal photograph of 1893. The boys are dressed in summer whites and displaying a fine array of plated instruments – the hornpipe dancer's straw 'boater' is seen lying on the bass drum.

The Wellesley was honoured by a request for attendance at the visit of King Edward VII to Newcastle in July 1906 – what a treat this must have been. Somewhere in this busy scene is the Wellesley band and a detachment of boys with carbines.

In November 1906 the band of the Royal Horse Guards visited South Shields to give a concert and the Wellesley band boys were invited. During the interval, the Wellesley band played an impromptu piece while the Guards bandsman watched from the audience. Mr Bilton, the Guards bandmaster, said that '*he had never heard lads of such tender years play with such ability.*'

The Wellesley band was so highly regarded that '*no combination of instrumentalists is more popular in the north than the clever band of the Wellesley Training Ship.*' An appeal was launched to raise funds to allow the band to compete for the Wood Challenge Cup, an annual event for juvenile bands held at Crystal Palace in London.

For certain occasions the band was engaged along with the Wellesley field gun crew. Naturally the location needed to be spacious and preferably outdoors. The crew would display their efficiency in unlimbering, positioning, rapid firing etc while the band, no doubt, played patriotic tunes to an appreciative crowd. One such occasion was the reception by the City of Durham, for Captain the Honourable Hedworth Lambton, CB, RN. At the end of the display Captain Lambton complemented Captain Baynham on the efficiency of his boys and said that he had '*never seen a gun worked smarter than they had worked theirs that day.*'

The gun was a 7 pdr field piece served by a crew of 18 boys. They would demonstrate the firing of the gun and would also perform physical exercise with and without arms, always accompanied by the band.

An inspection of the Wellesley in October of 1898 stated that '*rifle, cutlass and physical drill showed careful training and the field gun drill a high state of proficiency.*'

The Wellesley field gun.

The band leading the field battalion with gun.

In 1906, the band and field gun team were engaged on fifty occasions for such displays. They were even engaged by Newcastle United, to entertain the crowd at St James' Park on match days. What an absolute treat for the boys watching the mighty Newcastle free of charge each home game.

Above: Newcastle United, 1907 with the Dewar Charity Shield. Back: P. McWilliams and C. Veitch. Standing: A. McCombie, W. McCracken, J.Q. McPhearson (Trainer), F.G. Watt (Secretary), J. Carr, F. Speedie. Sitting: J. Rutherford, J. Howie, W. Appleyard, R. Orr. H. Brown, A. Gosnell. Front: J. Lawrence and A. Gardner.

NATIONAL TELEPHONE No. 32. EARLY APPLICATION IS NECESSARY.

BAND OF THE "WELLESLEY,"

FIELD GUN AND DRILL PARTIES.

BANDMASTER AND CONDUCTOR .. J. SHUTT (from the Scots Greys Regiment.)

The "Wellesley" Training Ship Committee have spared no trouble or expense in order to make their Military Band, consisting of 30 Performers, thoroughly efficient. It has been re-organised and much improved. The boys are dressed in Naval Costume and play on Plated Instruments.

Engagements can be booked for Parks, Flower Shows, Garden Fetes, Sports, Band of Hope Demonstrations, Ship Launches, Concerts, Picnics, &c.

The Music is carefully selected, being popular and high class.

A Hornpipe Dancer accompanies the Band when required, and a 7-Pounder Field Gun with a Crew of 18 Boys, can also be engaged at a small extra charge. They go through a highly interesting Drill with the Gun under fire, and give also Physical Exercise with and without arms, being accompanied by the Band.

Engagements have been fulfilled at York, Durham, Carlisle, Sunderland, Stockton, Berwick, Newcastle, and surroundings, numbering last year upwards of 60, to the satisfaction of all concerned.

I shall be pleased to quote terms, which will, no doubt, be considered moderate.

CAPTAIN H. BAYNHAM, ROYAL NAVY, F.R.A.S.,

To whom all Communications must be addressed.

The last word lies with the Government Inspector who wrote in a report of March 1900: '*The band is one of the best of its kind and must be turning out some promising young musicians.*'

Left: An advert from the Illustrated Guide of 1907 showing that the Wellesley band were available for events:

'Engagements can be booked for Parks, Flower Shows, Garden Fetes, Sports, Band of Hope Demonstrations, Ship Launches, Concerts, Picnic, &c. The Music is carefully selected, being popular and high class.'

Discipline

The year 1890 is described as the most disturbed in the history of Wellesley. The conduct of the boys was considered deplorable and discipline was regularly breached with punishment frequent and excessive. In 1891 Captain Baynham took command and the first task was to restore discipline and harmony to the ship's company. In its annual report for this year the committee noted '*as marked improvement in the tone of feeling amongst the officers, as well as in the conduct of the boys.*'

I have personal experience of managing boys within a controlling environment. Even though the maximum was only 45, this number was more than enough to cause major problems. Any institution operates effectively solely through the consent and cooperation of its inmates. When that consent is withdrawn then chaos ensues. The atmosphere within the building or in this case the ship can be brooding, expectant and threat laden. Sullen compliance can quickly change to outright defiance and it is then that the situation becomes perilous. Increased controls, discipline and punishment serve only to increase resentment against authority figures who become increasingly less effective in their role. In the case of the Wellesley even though the boys were not of criminal fraternity the potential for unrest would have been high. Naval discipline alone was not enough to tackle the multi-faceted needs of what in effect were children during their formative years. This was recognised by the committee and measures were taken to if not eliminate then to substantially reduce the potential for further disturbances.

Captain Baynham.

The ship's company was divided into five divisions. Four of these were under the charge of divisional officers who were responsible for the conduct, presentation and discipline of the boys in their division. The fifth and smallest division, numbering only 30 boys, was that of the ship's band and was under the direct control of the bandmaster. The officers were assisted by petty officers, comprising 2 masters of arms, 5 chief petty officers and 14 mess petty officers, all of whom were chosen from the boys themselves. While punishments were still meted out, the punishment book records far fewer incidents, with punishments much less severe. This may be due, in part to the awards system that was introduced. The number of 'bad marks' a boy had against his name was calculated each month. Boys with no bad marks were paid 4d each per month, with 1 bad mark 3d each, 2 masters at arms with no bad marks 1/6d per month, 5 chief petty officers with no bad marks 1 shilling per month and 14 mess petty officers with no bad marks 8d per month. This rate applied to all 5 divisions and the division with the lowest aggregate score for the month received a special award for all its members.

Captain Baynham was in charge of the Wellesley for around seventeen years. During this time his focus was '*to inspire the boys under his superintendence with the feeling that the ship is their home, that obedience ought to be from a sense of mutual trust and duty not the result of punishment.*' Mention must also be made of the influence of Mrs Baynham upon the boys. The introduction of a female staff member into a male dominated environment can have a startling effect upon its inhabitants. Conduct improves, language and attitudes moderate and competition for recognition through helpful deeds increases. An establishment can be transformed from dreary negativity which is accepted almost as normal into a state of positive vibrance. Captain J. McNab RNR Chief Examiner to the Board of Trade had '*no doubt that much of this good feeling amongst the boys is due to the kindly sympathetic interest taken in the boys by Mrs Baynham.*'

Visitors to the Wellesley

Visits to the Wellesley needed to be prearranged with the ship's captain. It was he that would give parties and individuals a guided tour of the Wellesley, explain its ethos and no doubt elicit as much support for the project as possible. Visitors such as these became a regular sight to the ship's company. Consisting of private individuals, representatives of similar projects, local and foreign notaries, and charitable organisations, most with courtesy of the day, returned a letter of thanks to the captain after their visit. These letters would have been a source of great pride and it is likely the observations were shared with the ship's company. Today we call it feedback; in gentler Victorian and Edwardian times such letters were a confirmation that the Wellesley was fulfilling its purpose.

Wellesley ship's company assembled on the main deck under arms in the 1890s. Members of the band can be seen on the roof of the deck house. All of the boys appear to be barefoot in true naval tradition.

Heia Heung Tan was a Commander in the Imperial Chinese Navy and after one such visit in June 1899 wrote '*My admiration of the discipline and general arrangement for training the boys is unbounded. Perfect cleanliness and good order prevails throughout the ship, and Captain Baynham is highly to be congratulated on his success.*' Praise indeed from a fellow professional.

A letter of September 1899, from J. Rushworth, Vice Chairman of the Rochdale School Board, reads '*We are pleased to record our visit. We were most courteously received by Captain Baynham and conducted over the vessel. The boys look healthy, and are evidently well cared for in respect to education and general training. The arrangements are admirable in every respect, cleanliness, order and discipline are excellent.*'

In October of 1899 three members of the West Hartlepool School Board recorded their thoughts: '*The ship is a picture of cleanliness, the health conduct and general discipline of the boys seem all that can be desired. We saw the boys at work at various occupations, and were highly pleased with the same. We wish to specially note the excellent quality of the food provided for the boys.*'

The Palace, Tynemouth around 1900.

In the same year the Right Hon Lord Charles Beresford, CBMP congratulated Captain Baynham and his officers and petty officers '*on the smart appearance of the boys and their cheerful look, and also upon the clean and efficient condition of the ship.*'

The Wellesley boys were also involved in fund raising for the Boer War effort in 1899. John M. Winter, Alderman and a member of the committee of the Tynemouth Palace Entertainment War Fund writes thanking Captain Baynham and his '*little men*' for their efforts at a fund raising event at the Palace. Needless to say, the Wellesley band was prominent. Mr Winter goes on to congratulate the bandmaster and to say that *'your little men won golden honours from everyone associated with the movement.'*

Writing from his home, Cragside at Rothbury in February of 1907, Lord Armstrong thanks Captain Baynham for sending him *'your admirable guide to the Wellesley'*. He goes on to comment that *'the whole of Tyneside owes a debt of gratitude to you for the high pitch of excellence to which you have raised the training on the Wellesley and the way in which you equip boys for the battle of life.'*

Lord Armstrong, Tyneside Industrialist and Chairman of the Wellesley Committee.

Earl Grey, considered the Wellesley Training Ship to be *'the first and most important manufacturing on Tyneside. It is the manufactory of character it has to deal with, it is a noble business and well and nobly accomplished.'*

A letter from Captain Daniell RN, while praising the Wellesley and its company, gives an insight into the daily routine onboard he writes *'Among the most striking and interesting features of the daily routine onboard is noticeable the choral grace for all meals, the God Save the Queen at 8 am, with the hoisting of the colours by the 300 voices together on deck. The morning and evening prayers with hymns, all of which are characteristically manned in true handyman style – a real treat for anyone to listen to and admire.'*

On the subject of the National Anthem, Captain Baynham had wrote a letter of congratulation to her Majesty Queen Victoria, on the eve of her birthday. In it he told her Majesty that the national anthem was sung aboard the Wellesley every day of the year and that he, his officers and the boys remained her loyal servants. Not expecting his letter to be acknowledged so quickly if at all, Captain Baynham was proud and no doubt delighted to receive the following: *'The private Secretary is commanded by the Queen to thank Captain Baynham RN for his letter of the 24th inst together with a copy of the Illustrated Guide of the Wellesley Training Ship.'*

Of course the outright winner for having a name followed by the most titles goes to Alfred Admiral Superintendent RNR, HRH the Duke of Edinburgh, KG late Grand Duke of Sax-Coburg Gotha who found that *'The boys under training appeared healthy and well fed.'* He went on to make a very short comment on his approval of the system of instruction aboard the Wellesley, which only goes to show that having a big name doesn't always mean having a lot to say.

AN ILLUSTRATED GUIDE
TO THE
TYNE TRAINING SHIP
"WELLESLEY."
ESTABLISHED 1868.
CAPT.-SUPT. H. BAYNHAM, R.N., F.R.A.S.
ONE SHILLING.
SOUTH SHIELDS:
PRINTED AT THE "GAZETTE" OFFICE, BARRINGTON STREET.
1907.

The cover of the Illustrated Guide to the Tyne Training Ship 'Wellesley' from 1907.

Captain Baynham received many such letters from visiting local and foreign dignitaries all of which heap praise upon the Wellesley and its company. These letters confirmed to him and his officers that the handling of the boys was correct, was beneficial and was fulfilling the purpose of the ship. It must be remembered that the boys were firstly, children. The situation onboard the Wellesley before the arrival of Captain Baynham has already been mentioned. It is clear from this that a regime based upon harsh discipline and overly punitive responses can breed resentment and disorder. While the late Victorian conscience may have been salved somewhat through the inception of schemes such as the Wellesley, the end product was intended to be used to protect a class system that was solely responsible for this need.

Britain, through industrialisation, rapidly became the world leader in manufacturing – particularly the

Tyneside based industries of engineering, shipbuilding and armaments, all of which were fuelled by coal from the massive Northumberland and Durham coalfields. Huge fortunes were made by the owners of ship building companies and industrialists such as Lord Armstrong, shipyards on the Tyne built warships and other vessels for many countries throughout the world.

Above, right: Built in Armstrong's Elswick Yard for the Brazilian Navy, the 'Minas Geraes' after being commissioned in 1910. The Wellesley can be seen in the background.

Right: The battleship 'Minas Geraes' fires a broadside of her ten 12 in guns. This is quite a dramatic photograph but it is difficult to imagine the noise. The 'Minas Geraes' was not broken up until 1953.

Recorded visitors to the Wellesley come from many of these countries and serves as an indicator of the prominence of the River Tyne in supplying foreign navies with vessels of war and commerce. The Japanese Imperial Navy, in particular was quick to recognise Tyneside expertise and quality in shipbuilding.

Above: The launch of the Japanese battleship 'Kashima' from Armstrong's Elswick Yard in March 1905.

Right: The 'Kashima' is seen here after painting and fitting out at Palmer's Hebburn Yard in 1906. She was broken up in 1924.

The Wellesley's Brave 'Littlemen'

Testaments to the Wellesley boys indicate a sense of comradeship that can only be achieved through a shared experience and purpose. In 1893, the boy T.A. Bell, aged 15, years was awarded the Royal Humane Society Bronze Medal for saving the life of his shipmate, J. Wilson. He had fallen overboard and Bell had jumped into the river fully clothed and wearing heavy sea boots to rescue him.

In 1894, Hudson, the son of Captain Baynham, fell into the river from the poop of the ship. The boy G. Smith plunged, fully clothed into a strong running tide and affected a rescue. At the time Smith was recovering from the loss of an eye. His selfless bravery was rewarded by the RHS Bronze Medal.

The winter of 1899 was particularly cold but this did not prevent J. Bagnall from earning his Bronze Medal. The boy J.G. Cummings fell overboard from a boat and Bagnall did not hesitate to jump into the river from a height of 20 feet to rescue his ship mate. His medal was presented by the Mayor of South Shields Ald T.D. Marshall who told the boy that he would be proud if he *'could exchange my gold chain of office for a medal like yours'.*

In December 1897, the boy W. Linscott fell overboard in bitterly cold weather and, with strong tide running, John Buckley, aged 15 years, dived fully clothed into the river. Linscott was a poor swimmer and Buckley could only hold him until a boat was dispatched to rescue them. When they were returned to the ship it was found that Buckley had sustained a head injury during the rescue. Mrs Baynham wanted to attend to him first but Buckley refused attention saying that Linscott was in more need. This was regarded as, not only a brave but also that which was selfless and noble.

The River Tyne was a constant source of danger for boys who fell overboard.

Only a Wellesley boy yet brave and true
we fain would give honour where it's due.
Such deed as these are Old England's pride.
As heroes in history page stand side by side.
He saw his shipmate sink neath the wave,
then plunged in the water to help and save.
Such pluck and daring thrills each heart.
John Buckley played a grand and manly part.
No thought of self, tho' the tide was flowing strong.
He saw his comrade life soon be gone.
His duty as a British lad was clear;
He knew not cowardice or fear.
Heroes have faced the loud cannons roar,
and have made their names ring from shore to shore.
To record such deed we are always glad,
and John Buckley is a hero tho' only a Wellesley lad.

The above incident and poetic lines were recorded in a letter written by Captain Baynham in 1903. He was prompted to write on hearing that a gold medal had been presented to James Buckley, brother to John, by the President of the United States. It is not mentioned why James Buckley was awarded this honour but Captain Baynham was eager to declare that both brothers were products of Wellesley training.

In 1905, HMS 'Cressy' was on gunnery and torpedo exercises in Lime Bay. The 'Cressy' was based at Portsmouth as part of the Reserve Squadron and was off the Devon coast when a sailor fell overboard. Attempts were made to rescue but lifebelts could not reach him as the ship was still moving and he had been swept astern. An old Wellesley boy, seaman Richard Wilson attached to 2nd Company Tyneside Naval Volunteers, jumped from the stern secured the seaman and held him at a buoy until a boat from the ship arrived. Wilson, on his Captain's recommendation, was awarded a medal from the Royal Humane Society. This old Wellesley boy was credited with saving 17 lives from drowning. A champion swimmer, Wilson won many prizes for swimming and would regularly attend the annual Wellesley swimming gala. He even managed to rescue one of the boys who got into difficulties during one of these gatherings.

Such heroic acts carry a high percentage of personal risk yet this does not seem to have been considered by the rescuers. The instinct for self preservation is inherent in all of us but these acts were not the reckless disregard for that instinct. They seem more like self appraisal, confidence, spirit and training. All of which were activated to produce an instant response to a dangerous situation. No doubt the captain, the officers of the Wellesley and the committee felt their efforts rewarded and the ethos of the ship upheld.

The ship's band play on the main deck, with the rest of the company mustered under arms. The little chap on the deck house roof may be the 'Hornpipe' dancer. Some of the boys wear shoes but most are barefoot.

In the previous 'Visitors' section of this book we had the comments and praise of those who had visited the ship. What of the 'old boys' who had long left Wellesley to ply their trade without the 'wooden walls'? The following letters were written to Captain Chadwick and published in the 'Third Christmas Booklet for 1917'. By this time the boys were being housed in the Palace at Tynemouth after fire had destroyed the ship at her mooring in 1914.

The following letter was sent from 'Somewhere in France', August 24th 1917:

To Mr Chadwick, Officers and Boys of the Wellesley Training Ship.
Allow me to express my deepest appreciation for the good time which you all – from the lowest to the highest – gave me during my short stay with you in the old Ship. It was but a short time, but it was, as the Americans say, 'Sometime'. My only regret was I could not lengthen my delightful stay with you all. From the bottom of my heart I thank you one and all.

It was a source of great pleasure to me to see how the work was carried out with the greatest precision and aptitude. The way the Petty Officers and Captains of Division handled the boys and formed them up when I made my speech called forth my greatest admiration. The whole system and organisation is wonderful. It is the outcome of determination and doggedness.

The Band is a credit to the Ship; stick to it boys, learn all you can, and you'll be able to make your place amongst some of the best in years to come.

Well done. Wellesley, well done all! I'm proud of the Ship and of the officers, but not least of all, proud to have come of the old 'Wellesley' stock. See to it that you keep the old name blazing as it does to-day, and in years to come your Officers will give you the grift of pride, that they did to.

Yours Truly, Albert Smith, DCM

On June 11th 1917, 20436 Lance-Corporal A. Duffy, D Company, 13th Northumberland Fusiliers, wrote to Captain Chadwick

Dear Sir
I received your letter dated June 4th, and was delighted to have news from the old ship. Well, in the first place, I must thank you, also the Officers and Boys for their congratulations to me on winning the Military Medal.

I have now been in the Army well over two years, a good part of that time I have spent in France, and during the whole period I have tried always to live up to what I was taught on the Wellesley Training Ship; its Mottoes, in fact everything I learnt have been of great value to me.

There are now a good number of the old lads who have won honours, and I know the discipline that they learnt as lads, has won them their honours as men.

Should I at any time get a chance to come across to England, it shall be one of my first thoughts to come to the Palace and see you, as I think I shall never forget those who were aboard the Ship, those who made the Ship a good home for us and did their best to send lads out into the world to become good men.

At the present moment I am writing this in a rest camp as we have just come out of the line, and not far away having a nap is another of the old school – he is cook for the Officers of the Battalion you see sir, something else I guess he learnt on the Ship.

Well I don't think there is much more to say so I must close my letter with kind regards to yourself, Officers and Boys of the Wellesley Training Ship.

I remain, Yours Faithfully, A. Duffy, MM

Private John Dunleavy, No 4 Platoon, 1st 6th Northumberland Fusiliers was a member of the British Expeditionary Force to France and wrote:

Dear Sir
I received your kind and welcome letter all right. Private Fletcher, No 3 Platoon, 1st 6th NFBEF, France thanks you for your Christmas gift, which he received safely. Your letter congratulating me on winning the Military Medal was much appreciated.

I am very sorry to inform you of Private Battista having been killed in action on November 6th. Well, we have had a good number of the old boys joined (also a lot we do not hear of) and, as you know you have only to get on talking about the Old Wooden Walls, or I should say, our dear old ship, and then you can tell who you are talking to.

Don't forget to tell the boys I am asking kindly after them, and I am very sorry I cannot spend my Christmas amongst them again, as I quite enjoyed myself last time I was with them all in the Old Boys' Mess in 1915.

Remember me to all the Officers and Boys, and last but not least, our dear Captain, who is doing his work at sea. Well, good night, and may God look over you all.

With Kindest regards to yourself, Yours Truly, John Dunleavy. MM

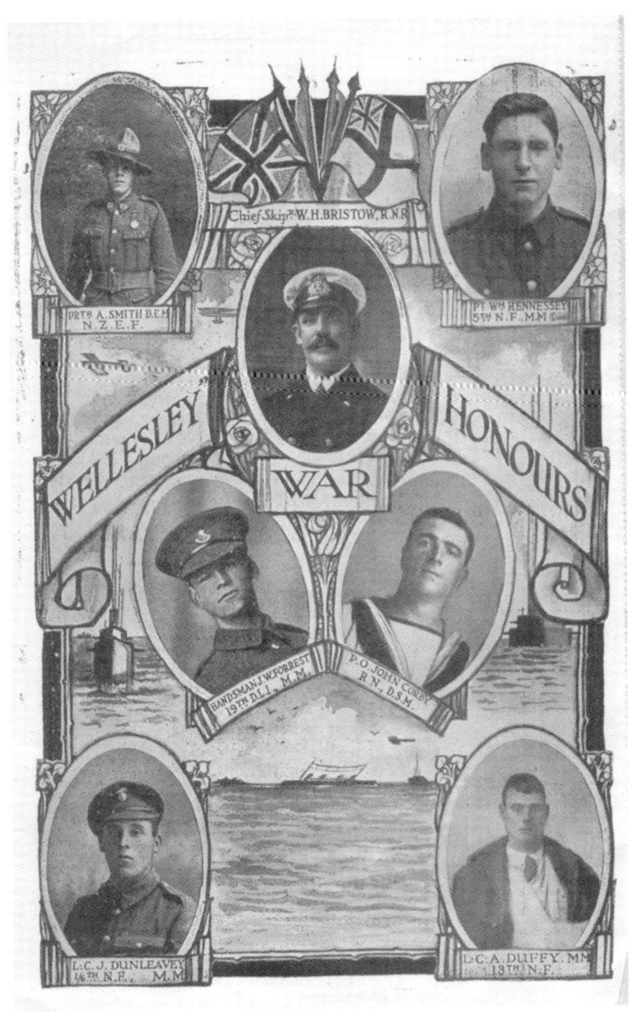

A few of the former Wellesley 'old boys' commemorated in the Roll of Honour.

Boys using a model to train for steering and compass in the early 1900s – how many of these lads were involved in the First World War a decade later?

Another member of the BEF, bandsman J. Forrest 'Y' Company, 19th Durham Light Infantry, informed Captain Chadwick in his letter that he was awarded the Military Medal on September 7th and was presented with the Bar, September 17th. Bandsman Forrest did not want to speak about the action he was involved in feeling that he was '*Only doing my duty for my wounded comrades*'. He also relates that Private Milburn, another old Wellesley boy, was wounded in action on the same day as he got his Military Medal. Bandsman Forrest was part of a long held tradition within the British Army. A musicians other duty was to act as a stretcher bearer and it was in this role that Forrest would have earned his award. Acts such as his were not uncommon during the First World War and, indeed many other conflicts. This one, however, must have been attended with a high level of personal risk to have warranted such a prestigious award.

Arthur Lane, Signal Boy, HM Yacht 'Sapphire II', C/O GPO, London. 3rd January, 1917

Dear Sir
On behalf of my ship-mate Arthur Wilson and myself, I wish to thank you many times for the Wellesley Booklet which we received on the 2nd inst.

On reading the book through, it filled us with delight and sent through us a feeling of great pride when we read of the courageous deeds some of the old comrades have done, and are still performing on Sea and on the blood-stained battlefields abroad.

We were also pleased to read how the boys now on the ship are doing their bit by making shell grummets and helping in many other ways. We were also delighted to read that another one hundred boys volunteered to join the Colours, during the past year. We wish them every success in life.

Wilson and I have not taken part in any engagements but are helping to keep the Trade Routes clear, thus enabling the shipping to be carried on.

I am anxiously looking forward to the 7th May this year when I shall be 19 years and expect to be rated Signalman A.B. and have my wages raised to £8 per month. Wilson and I are doing our utmost to get on in the world and so keep up the old ship's brilliant name.

We hope the Officers and boys enjoyed a good Christmas and if it's not to late, we would beg of them to accept our hearty greeting and best wishes for the New Year.

I think this is all we have to say at present. So wishing the Officers and Boys the best of luck, and trusting all are enjoying the very best of health.

I remain, Yours faithfully, Arthur Lane

Ernest Johnson wrote from Barrack 9, No 4 Loft, Englarderlagen, Rudlebed, Spandau, Bei Berlin. Ernest describes himself as a 'Civil prisoner of war' and writes:

Dear Sir
Just a line or two to let you know the old boys and myself are in good health and hope you are the same. Very pleased to say that I received your kind and welcome p.c. a few weeks ago, hoping you receive mine safely. Please pay my best respects and best wishes to all the Officers and Boys on the Ship, and also to Capt P. de W. Kitcat.
I remain, Respectfully E. Johnson

Another prisoner of war was Ernest Hall – a signal boy held at Afionkara Hissar, C/O Ottoman Red Crescent, Constantinople, Turkey.

Dear Sir
I have now got the privilege of writing a two page letter which enables me to convey to you anything which I am able to tell you under the conditions, and in the first place, providing my letter reaches you in time, I wish to tender to you my sincere greetings for a Merry Christmas and a Prosperous New Year. I wrote to you six weeks ago, and I shall always appreciate any letters you may have to send to me. I am now settling down to my new life as a prisoner of war and I have nothing to grumble about, only a desire to get home and renew the friendship of my various friends. I am in the company of respectable people who see that I get most things that I want, and that helps to keep me happy under the conditions. I am pleased to tell you that we have our Church Service on Sundays. There is a good choir which has been specially provided by our own men for the occasion. We are detained in a Church, formerly used by the Christians before the War. *I remain, Yours Sincerely, Ernest Hall*

The final word goes to Owen Riley of the Steam Yacht 'Morning' then attached to the National Antarctic Expedition. It is worth quoting the letter in full as it typifies the Victorian/Edwardian thirst for adventure. In it are names that have become famous because of the curious English mind set of considering a failure, a tragic one being even better, as glorious. To a large extent the achievement itself, especially if completed by a foreigner is outshone by the Englishman who gave his all, failed and often died in the attempt. Owen Riley writes to Captain Baynham on 23rd April 1903 from Lyttelton.

Dear Sir
I now take the pleasure of writing to you, letting you know that one of the old boys is in the 'Discovery'. His name is Thomas Williamson, RN. He left the old ship in the latter part of 1893, and I (Owen Riley) who left on the 24th April, 1897, am in the Relief Ship 'Morning'. We had many a good old yarn about the old times. He was in the party that went with Captain Scott's last depot, which was about 79 degrees south. He has done a lot of sledging and exploring the land, they have also discovered two hundred and fifty miles of land at the end of the ice barrier, and also found out that the ice barrier is afloat, and they have discovered a mountain which they have named Mount Discovery. It is in the Mac Murdo Strait, which used to be Mac Murdo's Bay, but Captain Scott has found out that it is a strait, that makes Mounts Terror and Erebus an island. The farthest south ever reached is 82 degrees 17 minutes, which was done by Captain Scott, Dr Wilson and Mr Shackleton, with sixteen dogs and six sledges. When he returned he had two sledges, no dogs, for they had died on the road south. They discovered more land down there. As for the 'Morning', she discovered an island in 67 degrees 30 minutes, 179 degrees 15 minutes east, that's all we have discovered. We shall have to come out again, as the 'Discovery' is jammed in the ice. So no more at present from one of your old boys. *Owen Riley*

Memories of Captain Hatfield

The following information is contained within a voice recording made by Captain E.J. Hatfield in 1977. He speaks to an interviewer but in places the conversation is muffled and certain words are indistinct.

Little is known of Captain Hatfield other than he retired from a lifetime at sea a Master Mariner. He tells us however, that he *'came from the homes'* and describes his train journey to Newcastle in 1912. The Captain had been born near Kidderminster, Worcestershire but was confused about the year. He thought that it was 1900 but discovered that his birth year was 1899 after applying for his birth certificate, to allow him to sit for his master's ticket some years later. In the event this could not be procured and an affidavit from the training ship allowed him to sit the examination.

Arriving at North Shields Station, the Captain then gives a delightful description of his walk from the station to the Quayside, going down the Tiger Stairs by the Tiger Inn, at Wooden Bridge Bank and then on to Clive Street passing the Seven Stars pub. Clive Street is described as being a bustling place *'full of smells, onions and all such as that'*. He describes *'flags of all nations hanging from the windows'* and it being *'only a narrow way through'*. The Captain and three other boys were escorted by 'Mr Everington', who had travelled with them. The ships at the dock proved fascinating but Mr Everington assured them that they would *'see a bigger one by and by'*. The Captain was congratulated by his escort for not crying at the prospect of what lay ahead. A dingy manned by boys from the ship came alongside the Fish Quay and the new boys were brought on board. At the head of the gangway if was necessary to sign the log kept for comings and goings and then to the ship's clerk, named as Mr Hagan. He had been a boy himself aboard the Wellesley and it was he that logged and removed all personal possessions from the boys. The Captain's three pence which he describes as *'a small fortune in those days'* was also taken as boys were not allowed money aboard ship. Pocket money earned aboard was given to the boys only on shore leave or holidays.

The Wellesley, with the town of North Shields in the background, as it would have looked, when Captain Hatfield saw it as a boy.

So far, the Captain had coped with everything with quiet confidence, until he was told that he would have to go to hospital. At this news he was frightened and cried as he thought that something was wrong. The precaution was taken with all new boys – a fourteen day stay in hospital as an incubation period against any disease brought onboard. On returning to the ship a medical examination was performed by Dr Gowan. After being *'kitted out'*, the Captain was put under the wing of a boy named Taylor. It was this boy's duty to ensure that *'you answered bugle calls, roll calls, learnt your proper place'*. During this period this boy was totally responsible for the actions of the new boy in his charge. It is obvious then, that both would benefit from a quick learner and as well as relationships within the mess.

There follows an explanation of the mess system and that it was unusual for the full mess of twenty five boys to sit down together for any meal. The band boys would often be absent from their respective messes as they would be ashore fulfilling engagements. On these occasions the band boys' meals were held back for their return to the ship. Captain Hatfield was no longer called by his name, instead he was given the title 'A8' – 'A' was his division and '8' being his number in the mess. His name was used only for official occasions. Each mess had two Petty Officers – one for each watch. The port watch was all even numbers and the starboard odd numbers. The number system extended to education. Odd numbers in watches throughout the ship would attend school in the morning and the even numbers in the afternoon. The evens would also attend the following morning with the odd numbers in the afternoon and following morning. Sleeping arrangements aboard Wellesley were what may be termed as 'Spartan' and would certainly attract attention of Social Services today – Captain Hatfield gives us insight: *'A tubular frame about six feet by two feet, with canvas stretched on it by head and foot lashings and side lashings of spun yarn through holes.'* This served as the bed on which was stencilled the occupants number. One blanket was provided and a horse hair pillow, both of which were stamped with the same number. The beds were folded and stacked each morning to allow the decks to be washed down. The lower deck or orlop deck was reserved for *'the habitual wet beds'* – enuretic boys did not sleep with the others.

As well as a night watchman there was also a Petty Officer on duty throughout the night. His job it was to *'rouse the wet beds at the end of two hours and see that they went to the latrine'.* Any boy who wet his bed was punished with a caning or a bad mark that would severely reduce their week's pocket money. Captain Hatfield had some sympathy with these boys for he felt that *'some of them were I think really physically handicapped and couldn't help themselves'.*

The tubular frame beds with canvas stretched on it used by the boys for sleeping.

Classes in seamanship were not as important as education and came third to tailoring. Every article of clothing was made on board and a knitting machine was constantly manned by a *'tailor boy, knitting socks'.* A boy's number was put into the socks by chain stitching and this was the same for every piece of clothing. Education was delivered in standards. Captain Hatfield is unclear that, *'There were three, four, five and six'* with no standard over six. There were examinations every year that graded performance *'just like ordinary school'.*

Seamanship was taught in what was classed as night classes. This would include drill classes in which rifle drill, sword drill and Swedish drill were taught. Swedish drill was simply physical training and as well as formal sessions the drill was employed to keep the boys occupied while waiting for meals. Boys would help to prepare meals under the watchful eye of an officer called the cook. Meals were prepared for the boys and the officers who *'had their meals on board the ship in their own special place'.* The officers and *'berth boys'*, who were trusted to fetch meals from the galley, generally served the officers' mess and keep their cabins clean and tidy. The berth boys were supposed to be changed each month but very often Captain Hatfield says were the same boys continuously. Mess cooks and *'boiler boys'* were changed every month but if they were proficient at their tasks, would usually remain. There were also *'dingy boys'* who manned the first gig and second gig. The first gig boys were looked upon as special as this was the Captain's gig. They had to be clean, well turned out and handle the gig in true naval fashion. The dingy boys would also ferry visitors to and from the ship, so not only themselves but the boats needed to be presentable.

Local traders delivered supplies and provisions to the Quayside at pre-arranged times and the Master at Arms would order the bugle to sound to call the dingy to its station. Bread was delivered every morning by Hancock's the Bakers. Captain Hatfield remembers that '*old Bob was the man, who came with the bread, and he was dead scared of the water and the boys knew it*'. As well as being scared of water old Bob must have been a kindly soul. He knew that the boys were always hungry so '*Bob used to bring them some baker's bread*'. The Captain calls the bread '*padge*' another name could be fadge bread. It was round and flat and could be easily hidden under a boy's uniform to be smuggled aboard for later eating. Old Bob had a little ditty he would recite when he got into the boat. '*How the boat aheed according to the speed and when you get alongseed I'll gie you some baker's breed*'. The second gig was bigger and the boys manning it a little bigger and stronger. They would collect the milk from the landing at South Shields every morning and take the empty cans back at night. Any trip that required going to the South Shields side of the river was undertaken in the second gig.

Captain Hatfield goes on to mention the band and how well it did under Mr Bowman, from South Shields. He mentions engagements it had, including the Red Cross functions where the band collected funds. Very often a contingent would accompany the band marching with rifles. These were ex-army from the Boer War but no bayonets were issued or allowed aboard Wellesley. Rifle drill usually happened before engagements where an armed contingent would be appearing. Cutlass drill also was held on the main deck but for the sake of safety, and because the weapons were heavy, '*single sticks*' with horn hand guards were used. A face guard and chest pad completed the equipment so little or no damage could be inflicted.

Attack and defence, with helmets.

As well as education, tailoring, learning knots and splices, general duties about the ship were performed by work parties. The ship had to be painted and kept clean. The white band on the ship's side was regularly washed and painted and the vessel generally kept '*ship shape outside*'. The work parties were changed monthly as were the boys who assisted the carpenter and the tailor. The Captain then gives a delightful account of how the band boys were selected. He says '*The Bandmaster used to look at your teeth, like a horse dealer to see if you were alright*'.

Captain Hatfield became a tailor boy, saying that he '*was a good tailor boy, even if I'm saying it myself. Because there were special things, like, officers wanted anything done to his uniform and that, it was always passed on to me to do, to keep clean for Sunday parades and such as that*'. After leaving the ship, Captain Hatfield made his home ashore with the tailor master.

The ship was centrally heated. The pipes running around the sides of the ship enclosed in what the Captain calls *'lockers'* – wooden trunking about one foot high containing, heating pipes and used by the boys as seating as *'there were no chairs or anywhere you could sit only around that'*.

As far as recreation was concerned the main deck was the official play space. Football was the main past time among the boys with the ball supplied by the tailor boys. Snippings and odds and ends of cloth were bound up tight into as near a ball shape as possible and kicked about on the main deck until it ended up floating down the Tyne. Recreation ashore was naturally popular with the boys as being in uniform earned discount on entry into places of entertainment. Entry into the Howard Hall *'for the pictures'* cost one penny. Anything could be brought back to the ship from shore leave, but not pocket knives or anything like that. Usually it was food, given by friends ashore; this was kept for you, to discourage petty theft.

In August 1914 the continent of Europe managed to almost self destruct. The Great War was responsible for sweeping away many comfortable ancient ruling houses. A few months before this in March, the all embracing environment aboard the Wellesley came to an end when it met the Nemesis of all wooden ships – fire! I can do no better than to allow Captain Hatfield to tell his story:

'Well, it was Wednesday; just the same as any other day – it was a rather nice day. It was the 11th March and it was my afternoon in the tailors shop. Now the tailors shop was forward down the starboard side, right in the eyes of the ship in the bow so we had magnificent view of the river and of the ships coming in and out of the harbour – you could see them all through the porthole. But of course, when it was your stint on the machines, you didn't always face the river. In any case, you had to watch more carefully, or you could get your fingers caught and suchlike.

It was half past two in the afternoon and the fire bell went. Now, continuous ringing of the bell at the main hatch was the fire signal. I looked aft and could see along the deck from the tailoring board that I was sitting on. I was especially attentive to the fire bell because I was hose boy for number 3 mess.

When the fire bell rang, I looked aft, and the tailor master said: 'I didn't know there was a fire drill?'

'There isn't a fire drill, it's a proper fire,' I said. 'There's smoke on the after part of the deck.' I could see it.

So he says, 'Go to your stations then.' I only had to come out of the tailors shop to the fore hatch and where my hose was. I had to get on the rail and unhook it and then run it down but I couldn't connect my hose because the cap, for some unknown reason, wouldn't come off. I don't

understand to this day why it didn't but my length of hose was never used. So I went onto the Delton pump.

We were lined up on the Delton pump either side. From half past two, to when we abandoned the lower deck (the orlop deck) where the Delton pump was, we never stopped. As one side of the boys relinquished the hold of the handles and stepped back, the others would be taking over, so the pump would be going all the time. We had a continuous rhythm and did it so often that it was more or less mechanical.

There were other boys who had old fashioned grenades – these were bottles in racks at certain strategic parts of the ship. Their job was to go and get these grenades from the racks and go to the seat of the fire and, on instruction, throw them in. They were full of chemicals that were coloured blue. They were about eight inches, globe shaped, and of course you used the neck of the bottles as a throwing lever into the fire.

The fire occurred in the drying room. The drying room was a place on the orlop deck, near amidships, beside the boiler. Heat was passed through clothes horses that were pulled out. All the washing was hung over these and the clothes were dried with the heat. Although nobody's ever said and nobody gave any real cause of how the fire started, but I think that the clothes or the materials that were on the clothes horses were overheated and caused more or less slow combustion. Perhaps, when some boy went in to take them out, it all flared up. We don't know, but that's where it occurred and it had a good hold when it started.'

Also in attendance that day was the Tynemouth Lifeboat 'Henry Vernon.' Later that year the Henry Vernon and its crew were to achieve immortal fame in rescuing fifty people from the wreck of the hospital ship 'Rohilla'.

The Wellesley after the fire, lying in the River Tyne.

Captain Hatfield continues by describing the abandoning of the Wellesley. He and others were on the orlop deck with the fire beneath them: *'They kept us there so long and then we were told to go up on the main deck.'* He describes tugs all around the Wellesley and then the order to abandon ship. The smoke from the fire was yellow because of the burning tar and pitch in the seams. With difficulty in breathing and stinging eyes, the ship's company abandoned the Wellesley in an orderly manner, leaving her to the flames. The ship was abandoned by division and Hatfield remembered that the Wellesley Captain's family went over the side just before he did. He names one of Captain's children, Phillipa ... *'Just a baby in arms'.*

The boys were evacuated onto any ship that got close enough to the burning Wellesley. Captain Hatfield found himself aboard the tug 'Vigilant' and from there onto the 'Satellite'. The 'Satellite' he describes as having more space than the 'Vigilant' but being cold and draughty. Straw beds were allocated to each boy and blankets that the Captain describes as being *'Small things, travelling rugs and were bonny colours.'* They stayed aboard the Satellite for two weeks while other accommodation was sought for the ship's company. During that fortnight *'We were all more or less infested with lice.'* The boys could no longer have their regular morning bath, so the baths in Saville Street, North Shields were often used. The cold of early spring was intensified through the boys being without their winter jerseys as they were being fumigated. The Palace at Tynemouth was secured as temporary accommodation for the Wellesley Company.

Captain Hatfield says that clothing, bed, bedding, lockers, equipment and *'such like'* were acquired and the Palace fitted out as best as could be, under the circumstances. As everybody began to settle into their new surroundings the month of August arrived and the 'war to end all wars', began. Further upheaval followed as the Wellesley Captain and most of the officers were on the reserve list and were called up to their respective duties. According to Hatfield all, excepting the school master, tailor master, wood working instructor, manual instructor and band master left. Those that were left had to extend their normal duties until gaps were filled with ex-naval men.

The Wellesley is seen in these two images, June 1914, having been retrieved from the mud of the Tyne. She is in a sorry state and was soon towed up river to be scrapped.

The recordings of Captain Hatfield recollections end here. He was to leave the Wellesley/Palace shortly after due to his age. He went into the Merchant Marine and retired a Master Mariner while in his 70s. Hatfield states that he had no regrets about joining the Wellesley; he had learned a lot but felt that he could have made more of certain aspects of life on board. Nevertheless, it is plain that he remembers these details with a certain amount of affection and even indebtedness.

The Wellesley was refloated in June 1914 and dismantled by Hughes Bolckow on the Tyne.

The Palace

As a result of the fire that destroyed Wellesley, the boys were hastily rehoused at the Palace, Tynemouth. The Tynemouth Winter Gardens and Aquarium had been built, with great difficulty, in 1877-78 at a cost of £82,000, a huge sum in those days. The 'Palace' connection to the Wellesley had already been established as the boys had attended entertainments there and the band given concerts. The building was intended to be the new Crystal Palace – making Tynemouth the 'Brighton of the North'. However, after opening in 1878 it was soon realised that the venture would fail as construction costs had been high and attendances lower than hoped for. The building was sold in 1880 for £32,000 and renamed 'The Palace'.

A fine view of Tynemouth Long Sands and Palace in about 1904. The cluster of bathing machines and shuggy boats show how popular this area was in Edwardian times. St George's Church Cullercoats can be seen in the middle distance.

In September 1882, the North East Coast Exhibition of Naval Architecture and Marine Engineering was staged at the Palace. This event was probably the most successful in the early history of the building. Every space was crammed with exhibits donated from all around the country. The 'Skating Rink' also (a small single storey building close by) was stuffed with ship models, marine engines and many other exhibits celebrating the North East maritime heritage. Much of the latter part of the century saw the Palace used mainly for concerts. Then in 1898 a Mr Graham acquired the building and began converting it into a theatre, eventually giving it the name 'The Palace Theatre'.

The Wellesley Christmas booklet produced while the Palace was their temporary home.

The new owners brought further entertainment in 1908 and audiences increased steadily until the onset of the First World War. With the coming of the war, the Palace buildings were required for use as a billet for troops of the Coastal Defence Force and as a convalescent facility. There was also enough space to accommodate the Wellesley ship's company, though not in the manner to which they had become accustomed, I suspect.

During the war years the number of boys was increased to 312, no doubt due to the extra space the Palace provided. It is doubtful that much could be removed from the ship as the fire spread and that there would be much worth salvaging when the Wellesley was re-floated in June 1914. Personal effects, training equipment, instruments, tools etc, could be replaced but the biggest loss to the boys was the ship. The Wellesley was 'home' providing security, knowledge, skills, comradeship and self esteem. The loss was tangible but the work of almost fifty years could not be allowed to go to waste. Proud traditions must be maintained, the ethos of re-claiming young lives and giving purpose, must continue.

It is interesting, to speculate what the outcome would have been had not the First World War cropped up. During their sojourn at Tynemouth the boys remained active both in the local community and in supporting the war effort. The band continued its performances at Charity Field Days, celebrations, concerts etc. In October 1917 the ship's band was treated to an entertainment at the Albion Cinema followed by tea compliments of the Tynemouth Parks Committee. The band had entertained visitors to Tynemouth in the park on sunny afternoons throughout the summer and a trip to the cinema was their reward.

In just over two years at the Palace, the band clocked up a total of 103 engagements with concert parties entertaining soldiers. The band itself and the rest of the boys were treated to a concert at the Palace by the regimental band of the West Yorks Regiment in February of 1917. They also attended the Military Sports Day of the same regiment during the summer where special races were held for the boys. With the annual treat at the beginning of August, a trip up river to Ryton, Whitley Naval and Military Sports shortly after and an outing to Whitley Bay at the end of the month, the summer appears to have passed off quite pleasantly. It was essential that routine and discipline were maintained and with some necessary adjustments this was accomplished.

The boys and officers on the steps of the Palace who were members of the 'Wellesley War Service Munitions Department. 1st October 1915 - 31st March 1916'. The notice in the centre of the picture states that 'Shell Grummets completed 83,700' and then shows examples of each grummet and the amount they had made. Two boys just below the notice are using mallets to place a grummet around an old shell.

Training continued, although having to adjust to the new environment proved difficult, requiring improvisation in true naval tradition. The Rutherford College in Newcastle and the Marine School, South Shields provided instruction for would be wireless operators. The South Shields Corporation Baths was the venue for teaching new boys to swim and lessons in life saving. As well as wireless, swimming and life saving certificates were issued for signalling, first aid (issued by St John Ambulance Association), metal working and carpentry.

Wellesley boys also contributed to the war effort during their stay at the Palace. Acting as stewards, some of the boys lent assistance at the sailor's home in North Shields were the survivors of shipwreck and U-Boat attacks were looked after. Others were attached to the staff of the Brigadier General commanding North East Coast Defences as messengers. The boys also did more direct work in producing grummets for artillery shells – 130,700 were produced by them between October 1915 and November 1917. Just as important as the practical efforts made by the boys was their effect upon the morale of the soldiers billeted in the district. The band and concert party were in constant demand to perform at regimental field days, headquarters entertainments and charity events. With the ending of the war in 1918, the need to count the costs and return to as near as normal life as possible was great. When those costs were realised, hundreds of thousands of British and Commonwealth dead, a weary population simply wanted to live again.

Right: Christmas Greetings from the acting superintendent, officers and boys of the Wellesley from 1917. At that time there 'temporary premises' was the Palace, Tynemouth. The acting superintendent was James Chadwick.

The officers, staff and boys of the Wellesley at Tynemouth Palace in 1919.

Final Days

The Wellesley ship's company stayed at the Palace until May 1920. After a successful appeal for funds, the boys were transferred to the old submarine barracks at Blyth, which became the Wellesley Nautical School. During the Second World War it was moved to temporary accommodation in Hamsterley Forest before moving back to Blyth at the end of the war. Naval traditions and training were maintained thereafter and 'Wellesley boys' earned a reputation for good conduct wherever they went. The Children and Young Persons Act 1969 brought about changes with Wellesley becoming a Community Home under the auspices of Sunderland Social Services in 1973. Wellesley closed in November 2006.

Right: Captain Don Swanston who led the Wellesley at Blyth from 1961 to 1980.

The Wellesley Nautical School, Hamsterley Forest, during the Second World War.

Letters from 'old boys' to Captain Baynham and his successors display affection and pride in a shared experience. It must be remembered that Wellesley boys had few, if any, family members to offer any kind of support during their crucial formative years.

Captain Hatfield describes the Wellesley as being 'like one big family'. He, like others, gained many benefits from his time on board that were to serve them well throughout his life.

The Wellesley boys and those of other training ships were part of a social experiment with its sights firmly fixed upon the economy and its defence. At the final analysis however, the greatest benefits came in the sense of personal achievement, self work, belonging, comradeship and duty.

Brian Godfrey

The Wellesley Roll of Honour

The following roll of honour was printed in the Wellesley Christmas booklet of 1917. With the roll of honour was the following message from J. Chadwick, Acting Supt:

'You can help me to keep the list complete by forwarding, as early as possible, particulars of any ex Wellesley Boys who do not appear on the Roll, details of their service which may be of interest, promotions gained, or any casualties affecting our Boys.'

Officers and Boys

Commander P. DE W. KITCAT, RN
Captain – Superintendent
C. CROSS, Instructor
S. LUKE, Chief Carpenter
A.S. MILLER, Manual Instructor
F. MUDD, Clerk
J.J. HAYTON, Chief Officer
J. MARTIN, Instructor
F. HOBBS, Cook and Steward
S.C. STANNARD, Schoolmaster
H. DESMOND, Instructor
F. STONE, Instructor
G.W. BOWMAN, Bandmaster
E. ELLIS, Schoolmaster

The list below gives the ex-Wellesley boy's name then his date of discharge in italics followed by his ship or regiment with any relevant remarks. Unfortunately, some dates of discharge are missing. The details printed here, are as they appear in the 1917 Christmas booklet. If any reader has any additional details please contact Summerhill Books and we will include them in any future editions of this book.

W. Absalom *Jan 15th, 1910* – 1st Bn NF
G. Alcock *Mar 19th, 1912* – HMS Conqueror
D.B.A. Allen *Nov 16th, 1916* – 3rd Bn East Yorks Regt
S. Anderson *Mar 19th, 1917* – 2nd DLI
H. Annan *Sept 14th, 1914* – 1st Bn KOYLI
R. Armstrong *Oct 14th, 1910* – 1st Bn DLI
W. Atkinson *Feb 5th, 1910* – HMS Queen Mary. Lost in Jutland Battle, May 31st, 1916
E. Avery *July 6th, 1916* – 9th Lancers

A. Bald *Feb 27th, 1908* – HM Motor Boat
G. Ballantyne *May 21st, 1915* – HMY Sabrina II. Discharged Sept 7th, 1916
J. Ballantyne *Feb 12th, 1913* – RNR Trawler Section. Later HMD Beatrice
T. Ballantyne *Jan 16th, 1917* – RNR Portsmouth
J. Balmbra *Feb 13th, 1912* – 4th Div RFA. Wounded in Action (twice)
H. Bamborough *Nov 18th, 1915* – RNB Shotley. Discharged June 12th, 1916
H. Banks *Oct 28th, 1911* – 2nd Bn E Lancs. Killed in Action, May 9th, 1915
T. Bannen *Sept 20th, 1916* – RNR Trawler Sect
F. Barker *Jan 18th, 1912* – R Irish Fus
J.W. Barlow *April 22nd, 1913* – RNB Devonport
G. Barrett *Nov 26th, 1915* – HMY Boadicea II
E.L. Barton *Sept 11th, 1912* – HMS Adamant
J. Basnett *Nov 5th, 1914* – 1st Bn E Lancs
A. Bateman *June 29th, 1911* – HMS Ganges. Later Discharged
A.E. Batey *Oct 23rd, 1912* – HMS Indefatigable
W.A. Battista *May 6th, 1913* – HMS Russell
L. Bearpark *April 11th, 1912* – HMS Philomel. Later HMS Empress of Russia
G. Beer *Sept 23rd, 1907* – RAMC
S. Belcliff *1898* – 1st Bn NF – Wounded 7 times in Flanders. Discharged from Army Dec 8th, 1915
J. Bell *Dec 1st, 1914* – HMY Verona
J. Bennett *April 22nd, 1913* – HMS London. Later HMS Indefatigable. Lost in Jutland Battle
A.J. Bentley – HMS London
A. Berresford *Mar 16th, 1911* – HMS Venerable
F. Berry *April 17th, 1913* – HMS Dominion
R. Bestford *Feb 10th, 1909* – 2nd Bn DLI
S. Bibock *1906* – Irish Fusiliers. Wounded (five times)
J.C. Bird *Oct 17th, 1911* – HMS Conqueror
W. Bird *1902* – 2nd Duke of Wellingtons. Wounded at Ypres
J. Birkett *Oct 23rd, 1912* – 2nd Bn DLI
C.J. Bishop *April 5th, 1916* – 1st Bn Royal Irish R
G. Bishop *Mar 4th, 1910* – RNR Trawler Section
W. Bland *June 3rd, 1912* – 15th Plat E Yorks
H. Bloomfield *Feb 23rd, 1917* – 1st Bn W Yorks
G. Bollingham *June 4th, 1915* – 62nd TR Bn
A.E. Booth *June 14th, 1914* – RNB Shotley
J. Booth *Aug 3rd, 1916* – HMS Ganges. Later HMS Augora
F. Botham *July 29th, 1910* – Royal Field A
E. Bowes *Feb 1st, 1916* – HM Aux Vessel Progress Water Carrier. Drowned. Ship lost at sea
E. Bowman *Nov 16th, 1916* – East Yorks R
J.V. Bowmer *Mar 31st, 1916* – 1st Bn NF
A. Bradbury *Nov 7th 1916* – RNR Portsmouth
A. Bradford *Mar 2nd, 1915* – RAMC
E. Bradley *Aug 20th, 1913* – 4th No Lancs
E. Bradshaw *Mar 15th, 1910* – HMS Apollo
H. Brearton *Dec 20th, 1913* – 21st W York R
J. Brennand *Oct 3rd, 1916* – HMS Ganges. Discharged Feb 25th, 1917
C. Brewster *May 21st, 1915* – HMT Water Priory. Later HMT Sweeper
T. Brewster *Sept 18th, 1913* – HMS Royal Arthur
F. Brier *Mar 17th, 1916* RNR Portsmouth. Later HMAT Viernoe
Hor. W. Bristow *Oct 9th, 1883* – Skipper of HM Mine Sweeper Sicyon. Mentioned in Naval Dispatches. Received Diploma from Admiralty
C.W. Brown *May 21st, 1915* – HMY Sabrina. Later HMS Anchor Star
H.A. Brown *April 6th, 1908* – HMS Africa
J. Brown *1902* – HMS Dominion
J.H. Brown *Oct 2nd, 1913* – HMS Royal Arthur. Later HMS Minerva. Later HMS Calliope
T. Brown *Feb 18th, 1911* – North Fus
W. Brown – HMS Dominion
L.H. Bruce – 22nd Prov Bn North Fus
W.J. Bruce *April 15th, 1912* – 2nd Bn DLI
A. Buckley – 3rd Bn DLI
W.H. Burgess *Aug 18th 1909* – 2nd Bn KOLI. Reported missing Jan 8th
T. Burnett *Oct 19th, 1910* – HMS Terrible

H. Campbell *Jan. 18th, 1917* – RNB Shotley
J.P. Capstaff *April 8th, 1915* – HMY Astrea. Later HMS Roberts
A. Carney *Aug 22nd, 1913* – 1st Bn S Wales Borderers
D. Carroll – HMS Albion
P. Carroll *July 12th, 1909* – 4th So Lancs
H. Carter *April 7th, 1910* – 5th West Yorks
J. Carter *Feb 15th, 1917* – 1st Bn E Yorks
R. Carter *April 8th, 1915* – RNB Shotley. Discharged Sept 9th, 1916
G. Cartwright *Jan 3rd, 1913* – Royal Marine A. HMS Colossus
J. Casey *June 19th, 1908* – 5th Bn NF
V. Casey *Oct 23rd, 1916* – 2nd Bn KOSB
J. Casson *Feb 24th, 1911* – RN Brigade
J.N. Cathrae *Feb 25th, 1915* – HMS Cyclops. Later HMY Medusa II
J. Cattista *July 28th, 1915* – 2nd TR Bn
A. Caveney *Feb 23rd, 1917* – 1st Bn W Yorks
W.H. Chadbourne *June 23rd, 1915* – HMY Mekong. Later HMS Duchess of Richmond
T. Christlow *Oct 1st, 1909* – 4th Bn DLI. Killed in Action, France, November 18th, 1914
J.W. Clark *April 10th, 1906* – ASC
L. Clark *Mar 11th, 1913* – RN Division. Later HMS Linnet
S. Clark *July 18th, 1916* – HMS Ganges
W. Clark – HMS Britannia
D. Clarke – HMS Britannia
J.S. Clarke *April 14th, 1917* – HMS Impregnable
R. Claridge *May 11th, 1914* – HMS Ganges. Later HMS Conqueror
J.T. Clegg *Dec 28th, 1916* – RNR Portsmouth
T. Clennen *Nov 21st, 1908* – 2nd Bn KO Scot Bord
J. Clinch *Feb 2nd, 1912* – HMS Hibernia
P. Clinch *Dec 4th, 1914* – HMS Marea
C. Coan *April 23rd, 1915* – HMY Sagitta. Later joined Navy HMS Glorious
J. Colley *Dec 27th, 1911* – 8th NF Cyc Sch
J.R.T. Collins *Dec 29th, 1914* – HMT Robina
J.T.R. Collins *Dec 29th, 1914* – 30th Res Bn North Fus
C. Collinson *Sept 28th, 1917* – 2nd Duke of Wellington
J. Collinson *June 29th, 1917* – RNR Portsmouth
T. Collinson *Oct 1st, 1914* – 2nd Bn DLI
D.M. Coltman *Oct 15th, 1914* – RNR Mine Sweeping. Later HMD Boyndie Burn
H. Connor – 1st Bn NF. Wounded at Battle of Somme, 1916
F. Conway *June 8th, 1910* – 6th Yorks Regt
Griffeth Cook *Mar 26th, 1908* – 13th Bn NF. Killed in Action, France September 12th, 1915
R.J. Cook *May 22nd, 1909* – Irish Guards
W.H. Cooper *May 28th, 1912* – 4th D Roy FA. Killed in Action, June 5th, 1915
Jno Corby – HMS Bacchante. Awarded Distinguished Service Medal
A. Coundon *June 12th, 1909* – 23rd Bn DLI
A. Coultas *April 22nd, 1912* – 26th Can Cont
T. Cowen *July 18th, 1912* – 14th Bn NF
J. Cowling *Nov 18th, 1915* – RNB Shotley
G. Cox *July 30th, 1915* – HMY Amalthaea. Died of Wounds, April 2nd, 1916
J. Cox *Jan 1st, 1910* – 12th Bn Ches Regt
W.H.S. Craig *Aug 7th, 1916* – 2nd Bn NF
N. Cranston *Mar 4th, 1913* – 6th Bn NF. Killed in Action, France, August 13th, 1916
W. Cross *April 20th, 1910* – HMY Narcissus
A.A. Crowe *May 21st, 1909* – HMS Victory
W. Crowe *Jan 29th, 1912* – HMS Formidable. Later Monitor Robert E Lee
J. Curran *May 21st, 1903* – 5th Man Terr
D. Curtis *April 12th, 1913* – SS Cymbeline. Drowned
C. Davidson *July 30th, 1915* – HMY Amalthaea. HM Sweeper Cleethorpes
D.J. Davies *May 6th, 1913* – 4th Bn DLI
E.K. Davies *Sept 21st, 1907* – HMS Brittania
W. Davies *Mar 22nd, 1916* – RNB Shotley
J.H. Dawson *Nov 19th, 1912* – HMS Impregnable
W. Dean – 1st Lieut Mine Sw London Belle
W.J. Dee – 6th Bn NF. Wounded and Missing
R.M. Dobson *Feb 25th, 1911* – HMS Juno
J.S. Donkin *Feb 23rd, 1917* – 1st Bn W Yorks
M. Donnolly *Jan 2nd, 1909* – 1st Bn DLI. Wounded, Battle of Aisne
T. Dorritty *Mar 9th, 1908* – HMS Agincourt
W. Douglass *Oct 2nd, 1916* – 2nd Bn DLI
H. Drew – 10th/3rd Aus Inf Brigade. Wounded in Gallipoli. Wounded in France. July, 1916
T. Dryden – 87th R. Irish Fus
A. Duffy – 13th Bn NF. Awarded MM. Wounded
T. Duffy *May 13th, 1906* – Royal Naval Div. Killed in Action, Dardanelles
J. Dunleavy *Sept 19th, 1908* – 6th Bn NF. Wounded in France
T. Dunn *May 29th, 1911* – North Fus. Prisoner of War
A. Dyson – West Yorks Regt. Killed in Action, France
J. Dyson *Feb 26th, 1916* – RNB Shotley. Later HMS Euryalus

W. Easson *Oct 19th, 1912* – 1st Bn DLI
G. Edwards *Feb 4th, 1913* – Naval Brigade. Was at Antwerp, now interned in Holland, 1914
G. Ellis *May 6th, 1909* – 2nd Bn Royal Berks
W. Emery *Sept 16th, 1913* – RNB Chatham. Later HMS Albion
J. England *Aug 3rd, 1915* – RNB Shotley. Later HMS Prince George

J.W. Fairs *Feb 24th, 1913* – HMS Queen
T. Farish *Mar 29th, 1915* – 14th R No Lancs
S. Farrell *Feb 26th, 1916* – RNB Shotley. Later HMS Royal Oak
H.A.W. Fayers *Mar 25th, 1916* – RNR Portsmouth. Later HMS Minerva II
C.P Fenthon – Royal Horse Guards. Awarded MM, Oct 10th, 1916
A. Fishburn *Oct 1st, 1914* – 2nd Bn DLI
J. Flatley *Sept 20th, 1910* – Royal Garrison A
J. Fletcher *Mar 20th, 1912* – HMS Shannon
J.W. Fletcher *Nov 16th, 1916* – East Yorks R
N. Fletcher *May 29th, 1911* – West Yorks
T.W. Fletcher *Sept 2nd, 1909* – 8th DLI
W. Fordy *Mar 20th, 1912* – HMS Shannon
J.W. Forrest – 19th Bn DLI. Awarded Military Medal and Bar for gallantry in the field, Sept 7th, 1916
A. Foster *Nov 15th, 1910* – HMS Inflexible
B. Foster *June 6th, 1908* – Cheshire Regt
C. Foster *Feb 23rd, 1915* – HMS Inflexible. Later HMS Laburnum
Ern. Foster *Nov 17th, 1904* – 19th Bn DLI. Sent to work at Munitions, February, 1915
H. Foster *Aug 2nd, 1913* – HMS Victory. Later HMS Osiris
J. Foster – 1st Bn NF
W. Foster *March 1900* – 1st Bn NF
E. Fowler *June 17th, 1915* – RNB Portsmouth
D. Frith *Oct 7th, 1910* – HMS Fishguard. Later HMS Empress of Russia
A. Frost *Jan 12th, 1917* – MF Aux Alchymist
F.E. Frost *Oct 3rd, 1910* – HMS Cambrian
J. Frost *Nov 9th, 1912* – DLI. Wounded in Battle in Aisne, 1914. Also at Hooge. Died of wounds, Dec 19th, 1915

J. Gaffan *Mar 27th, 1914* – 3rd Bn Lincoln Regt
M. Gallagher *May 5th, 1911* – Lancashire Fus

H. Garrity *May 27th, 1911* – Lancs Fus.
Killed in France
J. Gartry *July 18th, 1913* – HMS Achillies
J.T. Gates *Sept 7th, 1909* – 3rd Bn DLI
E. Gibbon – 16th Bn Royal Warwicks.
Killed in France, Dec 18th, 1916
F.G. Gibson *Oct 7th, 1911* – RNR Mine Sweeping
Sect. Later HMD Internos
J. Gibson *June 16th, 1916* – RNB Shotley
F. Gore *Sept 14th, 1912* – HM Aux Cruis Arlanza.
Ship sunk by mine in Russian waters. Saved.
C.H. Graham *April 14th, 1913* – HMT Wren HM
Trawler Andrew Marvel
W. Graham *Nov 27th, 1911* – HMS Natal
J.R. Grant *Nov 16th, 1916* – 1st Bn S Wales
Borderers
G.W. Gray *Jan 17th, 1911* – DLI Bantams
J.H. Gray *1901* – 3rd Tyne Scot. Wounded (five times)
M. Green *Oct 3rd, 1910* – HMS Lord Nelson.
Later HMS Kale
T. Greenacre *May 26th, 1909* – 1st Bn KO Yorks LI
W. Guthrie – HMS Berwick

E. Hagan *Nov 6th, 1903* – Royal Navy
J. Haisman *June 5th, 1909* – RNR Mine Sweeper
E. Hall *Mar 25th, 1916* – RNR Portsmouth.
Later HMY Zaida. Ship blown up off coast of Turkey.
Prisoner of War, Turkey.
J.A. Hall *Nov 4th, 1911* – Monitor Prince Rupert
J.J. Hall *Jan 26th, 1914* – HMS Ganges.
Later HMS Agincourt
F. Hand *July 27th, 1915* – HMY Sayonara
J. Harland *May 20th, 1912* – HMS Canada
P. Harlow *July 27th, 1915* – HMY Sayonara
W. Harper *Jan 1st, 1911* – 6th Bn E Yorks
G. Harris *Oct 11th, 1913* – HMS Newcastle.
Later HMS Robinia
H. Harris *April 13th, 1915* HMS Impregnable.
Later HMS Valiant
F. Harrison *Nov 16th, 1916* – 3rd Bn East Yorks Regt
J. Harrison *July 9th, 1909* – 2nd Bn Manch Regt
T.W. Harrison *April 18th, 1910* – 2nd Bn E Lancs
J. Harthen *April 15th, 1912* – HMS Duke of
Edinburgh. Later HMS Queen Elizabeth
M. Harvey *June 21st, 1916* – RNR Portsmouth.
Later HMY Valhalla
W. Hatfield *Jan 23rd, 1912* – 8th Serv Bn Ches Regt
J. Haville *May 21st, 1913* – NR Crystal Palace.
Later HMS Egmont
R. Haville *May 25th, 1917* – 1st Bn W Yorks
W. Hawkesley *Oct 1st, 1914* – 2nd Bn DLI
V. Heales *Feb 26th, 1916* – RNB Shotley.
Later HMS Courageous
W.H. Hearne *Mar 10th, 1917* – RNB Shotley
H. Hemsley *Aug 7th, 1916* – East Yorks Regt
M.J. Hemsley *Mar 5th, 1917* – West Yorks R
M. Henderson *Aug 7th, 1916* – 1st Bn NF
F. Henley *Mar 27th, 1913* – HMS Hawke.
Drowned in sinking of the Hawke, Oct 15th, 1914
W. Hennessey *Oct 8th, 1912* – 5th Bn NF.
Awarded MM, Nov 16th, 1916
A. Hessay *Mar 24th, 1911* – HMS Audacious
B. Hessay *July 18th, 1912* – Lance-Corporal Northd
Fusiliers
J. Hewison *Aug 22nd, 1914* – 1st Bn S Wales
Borderers
Z. Hickman *Aug 11th, 1908* – KO Scot Bord
M. Higgins *Dec 1st, 1910* – 2nd Bn Man R
W. Hitchen *Feb 26th, 1912* – E Lancs Regt
J.W. Hobson *Nov 26th, 1914* – RNB Shotley.
Later HMS Vanguard
E.R. Hogg *Feb 18th, 1908* – 3/7 DLI
G.W. Hogg *Mar 27th, 1915* – HMY Narcissus.
Later HMS Cormorant
J. Hogg –15th Bn NF

J. Holbert *Nov 5th, 1909* – 87th Royal Irish Fusiliers.
Wounded, Battle of Mons
A. Hold *Feb 26th, 1915* – RNB Portsmouth.
Later HMS Invincible. Lost in Jutland Battle
A.O. Holder Dec 1st, 1916 RNR Portsmouth.
Later HMS Glorious
T. Holmes *Mar 26th, 1914* – 4th Bn York R
W. Horrocks *Aug 3rd, 1916* – HMS Ganges.
Died June 29th, 1917
T.M. Horsted *Feb 26th, 1916* – RNB Shotley.
Later HMS Royal Oak
E. Houghland *Oct 16th, 1912* – HMS Indefatigable.
Lost in Jutland Battle
R. Houseman *April 8th, 1908* – Royal Field Art
F. Howitt – Welsh Borderers. Killed, Battle of Mons,
September 26th, 1914
J.W. Hughff *Dec 24th, 1909* – HMS Queen
E. Humphries *July 27th, 1915* – RNB Shotley.
Later HMS Prince George
J. Hunter *April 12th, 1913* – 3rd Manchester R
J. Hussey *Jan 16th, 1909* – HMS Suffolk
W. Hutchinson *Dec 12th, 1908* – 2nd Bn KO Yorks LI

T.H. Ingham *Mar 5th, 1917* – 2nd Bn DLI
J. Inglett *Feb 14th, 1911* – Royal Field Art
J. Inglett *Sept 26th, 1914* – HMS Impregnable.
Discharged

H. Jacks *June 23rd, 1915* – Government Chartered
Vessel SS Edie. Carrying War Munitions
J.T. Jackson *May 16th, 1914* – Highland L In
R. Jackson *Mar 31st, 1911* – HMS Suffolk
W. James *Oct 10th, 1913* – HMS Queen Mary
G.W. Jeffery *Oct 1st, 1914* – 2nd Bn DLI
W. Jelley *Feb 26th, 1916* – RNB Shotley.
Later HMS Marlborough
D.J. Jenkins *Nov 10th, 1915* – RNB Shotley.
Later HMS Albion
J.G. Jewitt *April 25th, 1917* – West Yorks Regt
W. Jewitt *Mar 27th, 1915* – HMY Mingary.
Later Highland Light Infantry.
Killed in France, April 14th, 1917
W.H. Jewsbury *June 23rd, 1915* – HMY Mekong.
Later HMT Cleopatra III
H. Johnson – Tyneside Scottish.
Killed in Action, July 1st, 1916
J. Johnson *Oct 17th, 1911* – HMS Neptune.
Later HMS Vernon
T. Johnson *Dec 5th, 1910* – HMS Monmouth.
Later HMS Vernon
B. Jones – HMS Centurion
J. Joyce *Sept 6th, 1914* – 6th Bn NF.
Wounded in France
J.H. Joyce *Sept 26th, 1913* – 2nd Bn DLI

W. Keeton *Jan. 11th, 1917* – RNB Shotley
N. Keithley *Mar 31st, 1911* – HMS Bulwark.
Drowned in sinking of HMS Bulwark
J. Kelly *Sept 30th, 1911* – Loyal N Lanc R
J. Kelly *Sept 24th, 1912* – HMS Queen Mary.
Lost in Jutland Battle
T. Kelly *Mar 31st, 1915* – HMS Revenge
M. Kelly *Mar 15th, 1910* – ASC
J.E. Kesterton *May 1st, 1917* – RNR Portsmouth
J. Kidd *Oct 5th, 1912* – 10th Bn NF
J. Kilroy *Nov 24th, 1911* – HMS Excellent
J. King *June 14th, 1913* – HMS Eclipse
A. Kirkley *April 12th, 1913* – 4th Bn W Yorks
J. Kirkley *Oct 15th, 1914* – 29th Bn Tyneside Scot

M. Lamb *1906* – Mine Sweeper
A. Lane *Nov 6th, 1914* – Flag Capt's Office
HMY Thistle
W. Lane *Sept 23rd, 1909* – 2nd Bn DLI.
Prisoner of War after Battle of Aisne
G.W. Langley *Feb 11th, 1915* – HMS Queen Elizabeth

D. Larkin *June 30th, 1912* – 4th Bn Naval Div
Alf. Laskey – 6th North. Fus
W. Laskey – 2nd Bn DLI. Awarded DCM and MM
T. Lawes *April 22nd, 1910* – ASC
J. Lawton *May 11th, 1914* – RNB Shotley. Later HM Submarine F1
G. Laydon *Mar 5th, 1917* – 2nd Bn DLI
J. Lea *Dec 11th, 1909* – Joined RN Hong Kong
M. Leavey *Aug 1st, 1905* – Seaforth High
J.P. Leckie *Oct 12th, 1912* – RNR Mine Sweeping. Later HMT Willonyx
F. Lee *Nov 21st, 1908* – HM Patrol Corinsin
A. Leith – Northd Fusiliers. Killed in Action, France, October, 1914
E. Lennon *Oct 31st, 1915* – RNB Shotley. Later HMS Blenheim
C.H.W. Levers *July 18th, 1913* – RNB Shotley. Later HMS Bellerophon
M. Levey *1905* – RNR HMS Pembroke
C. Lindow *April 8th, 1915* – HMS Astrea
R.W. Litchfield *Oct 28th, 1916* – 21st Lancers
G. Little *Jan 5th, 1910* – 5th Dragon Guards
R. Little *June 10th, 1911* – 12th Bn NF
H. Loughran *Sept 28th, 1917* – 2nd Duke of Wellington
B.J. Lycett *June 12th, 1911* – HMS Achillies. Later HMS Vestal
J. Lynce *July 7th, 1914* – Royal Marines
T. Lynch – HMS Suffolk

W. Mahoney *Aug 10th, 1911* – HMS Orviete
W. Marchant *Mar 19th, 1911* – East Lancs R. Wounded in Action, May 9th, 1915
J. Mardy *April 10th, 1912* – 2nd Bn DLI. Wounded in France
A. Martin *Sept 14th, 1912* – 4th Bn DLI
P. Martin *Mar 11th, 1908* – HMS Sapphire
C.W. Marshall *Nov 26th, 1908* – RNR Mine Sweeper
J.R. Mason *Feb 20th, 1909* – Royal Field A
Wm. Mason *Jan 17th, 1908* – RNR Mine Sweeping Sect. Tyne Trawler Control
A. Mather *May 29th, 1917* – 2nd Bn W Riding Regt
J. Mather *May 5th, 1911* – Tyne Commercial
F. Maud – 2nd RI Fus
C. McArdle *Dec 9th, 1907* – Royal Gar Art
H. McCarthy *July 2nd, 1910* – 1st Ches Regt
T.E. McCaw *Mar 19th, 1912* – HMS Powerful
Lost on HMS Monmouth, 1914
W. McClelland *Sept 25th, 1914* – 2nd Bn DLI
P. McCormack *1889* – HM Mine Sweeper Strathalladale. Discharged
C. McCormick *Sept 17th, 1912* – 127th Canadians
G. McFarlane *Aug 13th, 1910* – 4th Bn DLI
J. McGuigan *Dec. 7th, 1916* – RNB Shotley
F. McKenzie *Mar 20th, 1912* – HMS Shannon. HMS Prince Rupert
G. McKnight *Nov 8th, 1911* – Royal Field Artill
J.J. McMahon *June 12th, 1913* – HMS Diadem. Later HMS Hardy
D. McMullen – RNB Chatham. Later RND
J. McQueen *Aug 3rd, 1916* – HMS Ganges. Later HMS Euryalus
W. McQuillan *Mar 31st, 1916* – 2nd Bn DLI
J. McVay *Feb 8th, 1909* – 3/7 DLI
J. Michaux *Mar 14th, 1913* – HMS Hawke. Later HMS Centurion. Later HMS Indefatigable. Lost in Jutland Battle
G.R. Milburn *Oct 9th, 1909* – Y Co DLI 19th Bn. Wounded in France, Sept 7th, 1916
T. Miller *Aug 9th, 1913* – Highland L In
P. Milwain *Aug 13th, 1910* – 47th Canadians
W. Minkley *April 8th, 1915* – HMS Astrea. Later HMS Inflexible
C.B. Mitchell *July 13th, 1917* – RNB Shotley
F. Mitchell *Dec 14th, 1915* – RNB Shotley. Later HMS Leviathan
J. Molloy *Aug 27th, 1909* – ASC
F. Monks – Sub Lt RN HMS Viknor. Lost by foundering of vessel off Irish coast
Sharp Morgan *April 10th, 1913* – HM Aux Cruis Campania
J. Mort *Oct 20th, 1911* – 12th Bn Lancs Fusiliers. Killed in France, Oct 1st, 1915
T. Mudd – 12th Bn NF
T. Mullholland *Dec 12th, 1914* – HMY Verona

H. Nagel – DLI. Killed in France
G.W. Needham *Mar 5th, 1917* – West Yorks R
H. Neville *April 25th, 1910* – HMS Black Prince
C.H. Newbold *Oct 23rd, 1916* – 9th Lancers
C.W. Newman *Feb 19th, 1908* – 1st Bn R Berks
T. Newman *Mar 20th, 1912* – HMS Formidable. Later HMS Duncan. Later HM Submarine B5
T. Nichol – 1st Bn NF
T. Nolan *Feb 16th, 1912* – RNR Mine Sweeping. Later 22nd West Yorks Regt
W. Noon *Dec 22nd, 1909* – Lanc Regt

A. O'Boyle *Feb 3rd, 1905* – 15th Training Reserve
F.W. Ogilvie *May 27th 1911* – HMS Dominion
H. O'Neil *Nov 11th, 1910* – 2nd Bn DLI
H. O'Neil *Feb 25th, 1909* – HMS Nigella
J. Owens *Feb 16th, 1911* – RNB Chatham. Later HMS Vengeance

G. Parker *Aug 9th, 1911* – HMS Achillies
J. Parker *Sept 5th, 1913* – HMS Hawke. Later HMS Carnavon
J. Parker *Mar 25th, 1915* – HMY Narcissus
R. Parnaby *Oct 28th, 1908* – RNR Mine Sweeper
J. Parr *May 30th, 1917* – 2nd Bn Rifle B
Paxton – 42nd Black Watch
M. Paxton – Royal Scots Fus
A. Pearson *June 1st, 1917* – 1st Bn W Yorks
T. Pearson – HMS Bacchante
G. Peckett *July 2nd, 1913* – West Yorks
G. Penketh *Feb 11th, 1915* – HMS Bacchante. Later HMS Lord Nelson
M. Pepper *Oct 5th, 1909* – East Yorks
J. Pickering *May 4th, 1915* – HMY Salrator
T. Pickering *Sept 14th, 1912* – East Yorks. Prisoner of War at Dulmen. Captured at Fricourt, July 1st, 1916
R. Poole *Mar 10th, 1910* – HM Mine Sweeper No 40
A. Potter *1907* – 1st Bn Kings Own. Wounded at Ypres. Discharged – totally disabled
J. Powley *Feb 28th, 1916* – RNB Shotley. Later HMS Vanguard. Drowned
T. Preston *Feb 12th, 1912* – ASC

W. Raine *Nov 15th, 1913* – 4th Bn DLI. Killed in France, April 9th, 1917
M. Rawlinson *Mar 7th, 1913* – RN School of Music. Later HMS Monmouth. Drowned in loss of Monmouth
A. Rawson *Oct 27th, 1909* – 2nd Bn Leinster Regiment
A. Rear *April 18th, 1916* – 18th Bn NF
W.B. Redford *July 25th, 1913* – HMS London
J.H. Reed *Aug 21st, 1916* – HMS Ganges
R. Reed *June 16th, 1916* – RNB Shotley. Later HMS Revenge
J. Renwick *Oct 19th, 1909* – H.S Cressy. Saved from sinking of the Cressy, 1914
H. Reynolds *July 25th, 1916* – HMS Ganges. Later HMS Thunderer
C. Richards – 6th Squad RFA
J. Richards *April 18th, 1916* 18th Bn NF
G.W. Richardson *April 14th, 1908* – HMS Talbot
H. Richardson *Nov, 1911* – 1st Tyne Irish
J. Richardson *Feb 2nd, 1912* – HMS Cockrane. Later HMS Canada. Died
J. Richardson *Feb 2nd 1912* – HMS Pembroke. Later HMS Minosa

J. Richardson *Oct 12th, 1914* – HMS Pembroke
R. Richardson *Sept 30th, 1911* – 2nd Bn W Yorks
W. Richardson *Sept 26th, 1913* – 2nd Bn DLI
P.B. Riddle *Oct 31st, 1915* – RNB Shotley.
Later HMS Barham
F. Riley *Sept 21st, 1908* – HMS Viknor.
Lost by foundering of vessel off Irish coast
J. Robinson *1905* – 1st Bn NF. Wounded at Battle of Aisne, September, 1914. Killed in Action, 1917
J. Robinson *Mar 7th, 1910* – Royal Irish Fus
W. Robson *Mar 25th, 1914* – RNB Portsmouth
R. Rodgers *Dec 21st, 1909* – Wellington Barr.
Wounded (twice)
C. Rottgard *Aug 30th, 1917* – HMS Ganges
R. Rowe *Feb 16th, 1914* – RNB Shotley.
Later HMS Cornwallis. Ship struck by Torpedo, Jan 9th, 1917. Saved

F. Sadler *Nov 8th, 1909* – RND Anson Btn. Wounded at Dardanelles, 1915. Transferred to Munitions
H. Saunders *Oct 17th, 1911* – HMS Neptune
W. Saunt *Nov 24th, 1911* – HMS Hercules.
Later 1st Hants Regt. Wounded Ypres, May 11th, 1915
G. Scholes *Oct 1st, 1909* – HMS Apollo.
Later HMS Blanche
A. Scott – Government Tug
C.R. Scott *Sept 11th, 1913* – RNB Devonport.
Later HMS Silanion
T. Scott *Feb 24th, 1913* – HMS Marlborough
W. Scott *Nov 18th, 1915* – RNB Shotley.
HMS Cleopatra
J. Seales – RNR Mine Sweeper
J.H. Seery *April 23rd, 1915* – RNB Portsmouth.
Later HMS Emperor of India
C. Senior *June 6th, 1914* – 14th TR Bn
T.N. Senior *May 21st, 1912* – HMS Prince of Wales.
Later HMS Queen Mary
C. Sharp *June 21st, 1916* – RNB Shotley
W.H. Sharp *Mar 31st, 1911* – KO Yorks LI.
Wounded. Prisoner of War
F. Shaw *June 24th, 1910* – HMMB Irenic
F.J. Shepherd *July 2nd, 1913* – 27th Bn Manch Regt
G. Shipman – HMS Monarch
W. Shipman – HMS Africa
H. Shread *Sept 28th, 1917* – 2nd Duke of Wellington
J.P. Sibley *May 1st, 1917* – MF Aux Alchymist
R. Simpson *Dec 22nd, 1910* – HMS Queen
D. Skillon *May 21st, 1912* – HMS Cockrane
A.J. Skinner *Dec 24th, 1910* – Aus Brigade.
Wounded in France, July 22nd, 1916
A. Smith *Feb 13th, 1917* – South Wales Bord
Alb. Smith *Mar 19th, 1912* – 1st Bn WIR New Zealand EF
C. Smith *June 22nd, 1917* – 3rd Bn W Yorks
F. Smith *July 13th, 1917* – RNB Shotley
H.A. Smith *Oct 9th, 1914* – Royal Scots Fus
J.W. Smith *Dec 29th, 1914* – HMT Robina
J.T. Smith *Sept 14th, 1910* – So Aus Army Corps
L. Stell *Sept 4th, 1917* – 2nd Bn DLI
C. Stevenson *Jan 6th, 1905* – 9th Bn DLI
J. Steventon *Nov 4th, 1915* – RNB Shotley
J. Stewart – Royal Engineers
D. Stokoe *Sept 15th, 1914* – RMLI
W.H. Storey *Aug 14th, 1907* – 2nd Bn KO Yorks LI
H.B. Strong *Mar 11th, 1909* – 2nd Bn Essex R
J.E. Summers *Aug 8th, 1908* – RNR Trawler Section
J. Swatts *April 2nd, 1917* – 3rd Bn KOSB
Edm. Sweeney *May, 1907* – HM Transport River Forth
C.W.L. Swift *Nov 20th, 1913* – North Fus
V. Syred *Nov 30th, 1914* – Duchess of Connaught's Own Irish Canadian Rangers

E. Tate *Sept 24th, 1912* – HMS Queen Mary.
Lost in Jutland Battle

V. Taylor *June 23rd, 1915* – Government Chartered Vessel SS Edie Carrying War Munitions
W. Terry *April 18th, 1916* – 18th Bn NF
L. Thewlis *Feb 20th, 1914* – RNB Harwich.
HMS Shannon
H. Thorley *May 25th, 1914* – RNB Shotley.
Later HMS Impregnable. Later HMS Media
M. Trotter *Mar 17th, 1916* – RNR Portsmouth.
Discharged Oct 20th, 1916
J. Turner *May 27th, 1908* – HMS Hindustan
A. Tweedale *1905* – HMS Colossus
F. Tweedale – HMS Prince of Wales
H. Tymms *Oct 18th, 1911* – 1st Bn DLI

C. Ulstrom – 5th Aus Div
J. Underhill *Dec 12th, 1908* – 2nd Bn KOY

W. Valentine *Aug 8th, 1908* – 2nd Bn Seaforth Highlanders

H. Wager *Mar 25th, 1916* RNR Portsmouth.
Later HMY Aspasia
J. Wakenshaw – HMAT Sabreur
A. Waller *Nov 10th, 1910* – HMS Lancaster
W. Warden *Jan 13th, 1916* – HMS Orotava
F. Wareham *Nov 3rd, 1915* – RNB Shotley.
Later HMS Repulsa
D. Warren *April 1st, 1914* – HMT Hildaweld.
Drowned
J. Warwick *Jan. 11th, 1917* – RNB Shotley
W. Warwick *July 8th, 1910* – 1st Bn W Yorks
E.B. Watson *May 22nd, 1914* – RNB Shotley.
Discharged from Navy. Later 3rd Bn East Yorks R
J. Watson – North Fus. Died
A.E. Wears *July 22nd, 1913* – HMS Achillies
A. Westcough *July 10th, 1917* – 2nd Bn DLI
W. Weston *April 29th, 1910* – HMS Fearless
F.J. Whaley *Feb 25th, 1915* – HMS Cyclops
A. White *Feb 2nd, 1912* – RNR Mine Sweeping Sect.
Later 16th Bn North Fus
W. White *Feb 2nd, 1913* – HMS Canada
W. Wightman *Mar 25th, 1914* – SS Taplow. Missing
A. Williams *Feb 23rd, 1917* – 1st Bn W Yorks
H.G. Williams *Mar 16th, 1910* – HMS Calliope.
Later Royal Naval Division
M. Williamson – 3rd Bn KOSB. Wounded in France
A. Wilson *Nov 6th, 1914* – Flag Capt's Office.
Later HMY Sapphire II
E. Wilson *Aug 1st, 1906* – 2nd E Lancs.
Wounded in France, May 9th, 1915
E. Wilson *Nov 26th, 1915* – HMT Tafa-el-Bahr
J.O.H. Wilson *Nov 26th, 1915* – RNB Portsmouth.
Later HMY Boadicea II
J.R. Wilson *May 4th, 1915* – HMY Salrator.
Later joined Argyle and Sutheran Highs.
Killed in France, Feb 28th, 1917
N. Wilson *April 8th, 1916* – West Yorks Reg
T. Wilson *April 6th, 1911* – HMS Maidstone
W. Wilson *May 23rd, 1900* – 14th Bn NF
W.G. Wilson *April 25th, 1910* – HMS Leviathian
E.H. Winley *July 25th, 1916* – HMS Ganges.
Later HMS Thunderer
R. Winter *Sept 3rd, 1913* – Tyneside Scottish.
Discharged – under age. Later 12th NF. Wounded in France
A. Wood *May 11th, 1908* – HMS Renown. Later HMS Hampshire. Wounded in Jutland Battle
R. Wood *Oct 13th, 1910* – 6th Bn NF. Wounded at Battle of Somme, 1916. Died of wounds, France
R. Wood *July 25th, 1913* – Royal Gar Art
W.G. Wood *Dec 14th, 1910* – KOSB. Killed
S. Workman *Sept 18th, 1909* – 37th Div RFA
H. Worsop *June 4th, 1915* – HMS Caesar

A. Yallop *June 19th, 1917* – 3rd Bn W Yorks

Civil Prisoners of War

M. Absalom *May 20th, 1911* – 2nd Bn Tyneside Scottish
R. Allen *May 23rd, 1912* – 15th Bn NF
Hy. Andrews *Oct 2nd, 1914* – DLI. Wounded at Ypres
G. Armfield *Oct 5th, 1911* – 2/1 Monmouth Regt
A. Armstrong – East Yorks

J.G. Battister – 6th Bn NF. Killed in France, Nov 5th, 1916
J.W. Baxter *Mar 19th, 1914* – 18th Bn West Yorks
J.W. Bell *Feb 6th, 1914* – Royal Engineers IWT
H. Berry *Feb 20th, 1912* – 3rd Bn NF
J. Betts *July 3rd, 1908* – 3rd Bn DLI
G. Birdsall *1908* – 2nd RI Fus. Wounded in France
T. Bone *Dec 23rd, 1909* – 4th Bn NF
J.P. Brierley *May 29th, 1912* – 14th Bn NF
H. Brindley *June 6th, 1912* – SS Falls of Orchy
T. Bullock *Feb 19th, 1914* – 4th Bn Ches R
E. Burrell *Nov 22nd, 1915* – 1st Bn DLI

J. Carlyle *April 1st, 1914* – Royal Field A
J. Carter *April 7th, 1910* – 5th Bn West Yorks. Wounded in France
J.H. Chambers *July 13th, 1912* – 3rd Bn NF
H. Clarke *Aug 9th, 1913* – York and Lancs Regt. Killed at Mons, Dec 1st, 1915
J. Copeland *May 4th, 1912* – Royal Engineers
A. Cox *Dec 4th, 1914* – 18th Regt London Ir
C.E. Crowell *April 12th, 1913* – 17th Bn Welsh Regt

J.P. Davison *Mar 3rd, 1913* – Tyneside Scot
E. Dennis *Jan 24th, 1917* – SS Brecknockshire
A. Dick – 1st RI Fus
J. Drew *March, 1906* – Royal Field A

J.W. Elliott *Feb, 1911* – 7th Bn DLI. Killed in France, Aug 27th, 1915

T.F. Ferguson *Sept 17th, 1913* – 6th Bn NF. Wounded
C. Firman *Sept 8th, 1913* – 5th Bn Royal Eng
G. Fletcher – 1/6 North Fus
Newark Foster *Mar 12th, 1900* – 1st Bn NF

E. Gatenby *Dec 9th, 1910* – 8th Bn NF. Killed in Gallipoli, Sept 19th, 1915
E. Gibbon *Mar 5th, 1914* – 19th Bn DLI
F. Godber *Mar 20th, 1914* – 3/7th Sher For
R. Goldsworthy *Oct 8th, 1912* – 5th Bn NF. Killed in France, Nov 1st, 1916
W. Gore *Dec 8th, 1910* – 3rd Bn Ches R
J.W. Goughlan *Jan 19th, 1903* – 2nd RI Fus. Wounded in Flanders

H.C. Hackett *Mar 12th, 1914* – SS President
E.E. Hall *Oct 23rd, 1915* – 3rd Bn Yorks R
A. Halliday *June 23rd, 1914* – 7th Bn DLI
J. Harrison *Jan 27th, 1903* – Sg Mag Royal Berks. Killed La Basse, Aug 20th, 1915
Jas Henderson – 6th Bn NF
E.R. Hogg *Feb 18th, 1908* – 7th Bn DLI
J. Huthwaite *Sept 28th, 1915* – 1st Bn NF

E. Johnson *April 28th, 1914* – SS President. Released, Aug 6th, 1915
J. Johnson – 1st Bn NF. Wounded and missing

J. Kerr *Aug 15th, 1913* – 29th Res Bn North Fus
G. Kilroy *Nov 19th, 1911* – 1st Bn Royal Scots
Jno Kirk *July 19th, 1911* – North Field A. Wounded (twice)

P.L. Lancaster *Nov 22nd, 1915* – 2nd Bn DLI
J.T. Lawton *Dec 14th, 1914* – 9th Bn South Lancs. Wounded in retreat from Servia
J.T. Lee *April 24th, 1910* – ASC
J. Long *May 11th, 1910* – 4th Bn AE Force. Died of Wounds, May 18th, 1916
N.G. Lorraine *June 16th, 1913* – Royal West Kent Regt. Wounded at Battle of the Somme (twice)
G. Lovett *Aug 30th, 1912* – 15th Bn Sher For

M. Maddison *Feb 21st, 1914* – Royal Field A
B. Martin *June 18th, 1913* – 3rd Bn LN Lancs
R. Maskill *June 6th, 1914* – 17th Bn West Yorks
J.A. McCaw *Oct 1st, 1913* – 3/4 North Fus
H. McGuigan *Jan 29th, 1916* – 9th Lancers
H. McKenna *May 23rd, 1911* – 5th Bn NF
J. McMaster *May 11th, 1894* – 3rd Bn NF
M. McMaster *Feb 12th, 1897* – 6th Bn NF
A. McMullen *April 23rd, 1910* – 3rd Bn 16th Hamp Regt
D. McMullen *June 1st, 1908* – 2/4 NF How B
J. Monoghan *Dec 1886* – 2nd Bn NF
N. Mulholland *Nov 22nd, 1915* – 2nd Bn DLI
A. Mullen *Mar 20th, 1913* – 3/4 RFA

J. Nelson *Dec 31st, 1910* – Australian Exped Force
W. Newham *May 29th, 1908* – SS Beneficient
T. Nichol *Nov 17th, 1900* – 1st Bn NF

W. Parker *Oct 19th, 1905* – 2nd Border Regt. Killed in Action, Oct 25th, 1914
J. Parry *April 14th, 1911* – 4th Bn NF. Wounded in France
A. Phillips *April 14th, 1913* – 7th Bn DLI. Wounded in France
J.B. Pocock *1895* – 6th Bn NF
J. Purvis *Nov 3rd, 1909* – Prince of Wales Own Yorks

M. Ramsey *Feb 16th, 1912* – RAMC

D. Seymour *May 21st, 1909* – 5th Bn NF
G. Shand *April 29th, 1913* – 6th North Fus
T. Shuttleworth *Aug 27th, 1913* – 6th Bn Worcester. Wounded
W.D. Skeet *July 2nd, 1913* 24th Bn Queen's Regt
J. Skelly *May 30th, 1910* – Royal Field A
J. Smiles *Mar 18th, 1910* – 6th Bn NF
H. Standring *Jan 28th, 1914* – 24th Bn Man R
D. Stokoe *Sept 15th, 1914* – 6th Bn NF
H. Sutherland *Mar 12th, 1900* – 1st Bn NF
J.W. Sweetman *June 9th, 1914* – 3rd Border Regt

T. Thacker *Aug 10th, 1912* – 3rd Bn NF
J. Thompson *Aug 27th, 1913* – 13th Bn York R. Wounded in France
Leo. Thompson *Nov 19th, 1915* – 1st Bn NF
J.A. Tolan *Aug 27th, 1913* – Bantams DLI
J.T. Turnbull *Oct 13th, 1915* – 3rd Bn E Yorks

R. Wainwright – 3rd Bn DLI
C. Weatherhead *May 31st, 1912* – 19th Bn DLI
W.E. Wilson *April 23rd, 1912* – Royal Field A
G. Woods *Nov 8th, 1915* – 2/4 Bn East Yorks

Also available from Summerhill Books

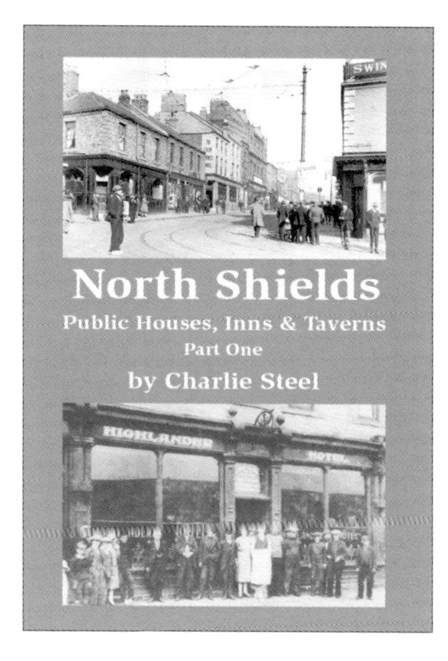

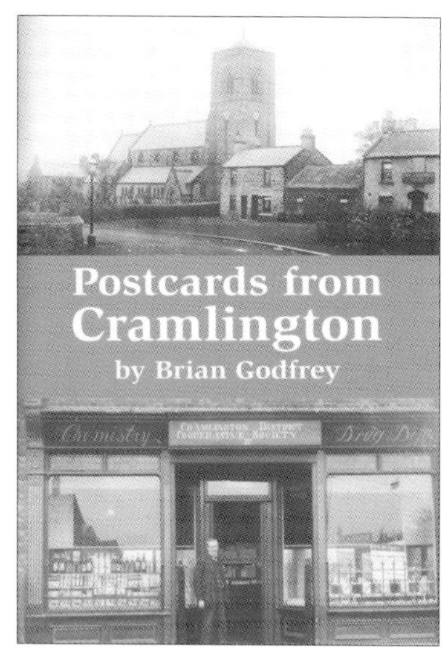

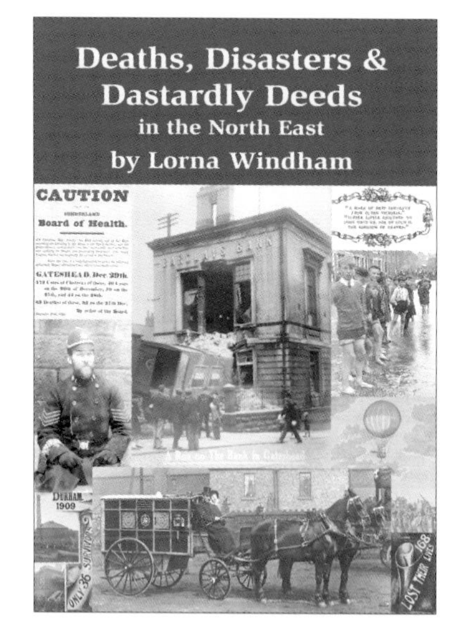

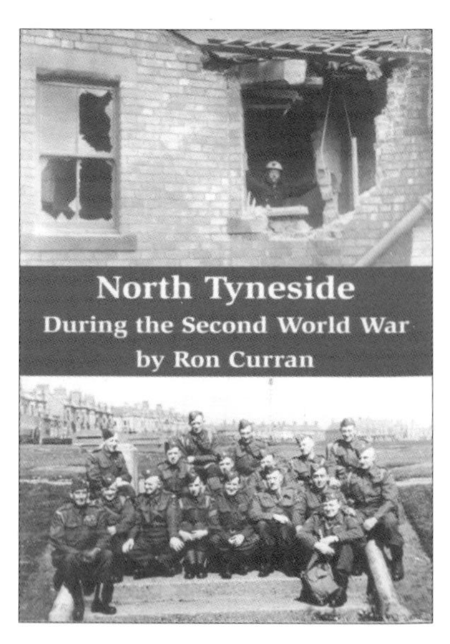

www.summerhillbooks.co.uk